Washington DC: Streets and Statues

Statues

Walking in the Steps of History

Mark N. Ozer

DEDICATION

For my children and grandchildren who provided the incentive to make history come alive.

TABLE OF CONTENTS

ACKNOWLEDGEMENTS

This book arose out of my long standing interest in how American history and geography manifest themselves in the rational order of the streets of Washington. As a Bostonian by birth and nurture, my residence in Washington has amazed me as to its rationality; so unlike the seemingly haphazard street scheme of my native city. Many of the names are the same; they reflect the strong influence of New England on the political, military and cultural history of the early republic now enshrined as Washington's street names. However, I was especially pleased to learn that Alexander Hagner was inspired to suggest in the 1890s the naming of Washington's streets after the alphabetized streets of Boston's Back Bay.

My earlier efforts to seek the basis for the names on the streets in Northwest Washington were included in my 2011 book by History Press Northwest Washington: Tales from West of the Park. These efforts were further amplified by work done on behalf of Rona Hartman. A good friend, she also encouraged the publication over several years of articles about the street names of Cleveland Park in the Newsletter of the Cleveland Park Historical Society that she edits.

I am particularly indebted to the work of William Goode in his monumental books on Washington's outdoor sculpture. I have been more selective than his encyclopedic efforts so as not to attempt to duplicate them. Once again, I have tried to be original by choosing to reflect the temporal context in which certain figures were memorialized as well as those who were chosen. My suggestion is that that temporal sequence is worth noting. I have also drawn from my own interests in exploring more deeply in some instances the political and historical contexts from which some of these figures arose. These efforts reflect my own interest in the Civil War nurtured by teaching at the Osher Lifelong Learning Institute at American University and a Civil War Discussion Group founded at the Cosmos Club.

I am particularly indebted to the staff of the Map and Geography Division of the Library of Congress for their help in finding the maps that I hope convey the vision of Peter L'Enfant in the 1790s that found fruition in the 1990s; and to Donald Hawkins for access to the map of the original "Ferry Road". Matthew Wallis has been helpful in working on the figures. The figures are drawn from the Library of Congress.

INTRODUCTION

The United States of America is a government unique in history as the modern world's first successful rebellion against colonialism dedicated to the principles of political independence and individual liberty. It was not only a new country but a new kind of country in the New World. Its leaders had the ambition to create a city to be its Seat of Government "worthy of a great empire" but also symbolic of its founding principles.

The creative effort that marked the Constitution was followed almost immediately by the design of a new community to translate the separate powers described in the Constitution into physical space with the Legislature enshrined on a hill and the Executive somewhat less prominent at a distance away. The streets of the city mirrored the Federalist vision of a central government with broad avenues radiating from the major public buildings providing "vistas extending into the distance." Order was further imposed by streets numbered and alphabetized all emanating from the central focus of the U.S. Capitol that also divided the city into the four quadrants of the compass. The Mall, L'Enfant's "Grand Avenue," united the two major public buildings by a projected statue of the country's founder. The grandeur now finally achieved by its monuments was long preceded in the 19th century by the street design that awaited its completion in the 20th century.

The original City of Washington laid out by Peter L'Enfant covered the coastal plain between the two branches of the Potomac River. Tiber Creek was a major dividing line between the two centers of population that grew up around the Legislative and Executive powers precariously connected by Pennsylvania Avenue as it skirted its marshy border. The growth of the city during and after the Civil War finally began to fill in the skeleton laid out so grandly at the start.

The growth of the city above the coastal plain onto the surrounding hills made necessary different foci for the organization of the city. Rock Creek became the natural dividing line between the much expanded city encompassing the entire District of Columbia. The important original east-west connection between the two major public buildings was transformed into movement along the north-south corridors. Seventh Street and Fourteenth Street was joined with Sixteenth Street as the last became the major spine leading from the White House north to the apex of the District. In the west, Connecticut Avenue joined the earlier High Street that became Wisconsin Avenue.

Starting on the lower and less steep hills on the east and then on the higher and steeper hills in the west, horse cars and then electrified trolleys brought development along the streets still numbered in relation to the U.S. Capitol or avenues now named after the larger number of states. More problematical was the naming of the east-west streets. The names given to the second and then third tier extended the principle of a city reflecting both American history and the American countryside that underlay the original design reflecting the Constitution and the geography of the original states.

L'Enfant's original design with diagonal avenues crossing a rectangular grid he envisaged as providing circles and squares to be developed by each of the then fifteen states. He thought it fitting that "statues, columns and obelisks" be erected as appropriate for each state. Although the plan was never accomplished, the numerous circles and parklets his plan created awaited the installation of stone and bronze memorials of great figures. The commemoration of great military and political figures has proceeded during the past two hundred years.

The generation after the Civil War saw the great proliferation of equestrian statues of military figures commemorating that great watershed of the American nation. Increasingly in the 20h century, focus has shifted from heroic figures on horseback to enumerating the names of those who fought. There has also been an increased admixture of other American figures of note; and, after World War II, with the increased international stature of the United States, representation of figures from the entire world who also share in the American dream of political independence and individual liberty.

Who are the persons whose familiar names are part of our everyday lives as we live and visit on the streets of Washington? Why are they there? This book deals with the design of the city to reflect its purpose as the capital city of a great country to embody that country and its history; and then of its subsequent role as a world capital to reflect the principles that make it so important to people the world over. The first major section describes the component parts of the street scheme, the second section the figures from American history and places in the American countryside before the third section describes many of the important political and military figures commemorated in the statues on its public streets.

SECTION I
THE COMPONENT FEATURES

INTRODUCTION

The evolution of Washington and the District of Columbia over the past two centuries first incorporated the original city on the coastal plain designed by Peter L'Enfant in the 1790s. A street scheme consisted of broad avenues commemorating the component states and their geographic position in the country upon which was superimposed a rectangular grid. North-south streets numbered and east-west streets alphabetized were in reference to the central focus of the U.S. Capitol. Grand as it was, the entire expanse between the Potomac and its Eastern Branch filled out only during and after the Civil War. The Tiber Creek and the Washington Canal remained the natural dividing line until development began to occur in the hills to the north surrounding the original town.

Enabled by the electrified street railways at the turn of the 20th century, population increased in the hills to the north in the remainder of the District of Columbia. Development occurred first without reference to the original grand design. The street scheme of north-south numbered streets could be easily maintained; avenues could be extended and others added. However, problems particularly arose in dealing with the east-west streets as distances increased. Finally, a street scheme was devised that maintained the original aim for the national capital to reflect the history and geography of the country as a whole.

The original focus on connecting the areas of settlement east and west of Tiber Creek shifted with the diffusion of population north of the original central core. North-south arterial streets became more prominent. Division of the area shifted to that created by Rock Creek that flows north-south from the District Line to the Potomac amplified by the maintenance of its natural state as an urban park. The street scheme that was devised recognizes this north-south division by Rock Creek along with division into four quadrants so that the each street is not duplicated.

CHAPTER 1
THE CITY OF WASHINGTON

Before there was a City of Washington in the District of Columbia in 1790, there was in the 1750s a Georgetown in Montgomery County in the colony of Maryland. Before there was a Georgetown, there were land grants called "Rock Creek Plantation" and "Rock of Dunbarton" and a trail that crossed the river then called the "Potawomeck." The Piscataway and Powhatan Indian federations of tribes that lived along the river mainly depended on the waterways for transportation. They also walked trails lightly in the 17th century before there were rolling roads that carried tobacco to be exported at the port of Georgetown.

1.1 The Early Roads

One important east-west Indian trail crossed the Potomac from the southern shore to the island at the mouth of Rock Creek and then across the wider channel to the northern shore. From there an east-west trail crossed Rock Creek skirting the river on higher ground to the point in the east where a ferry crossed the Eastern Branch named by the visiting Jesuits after the Anacostan local tribe (see Figure 1 "The Ferry Road").

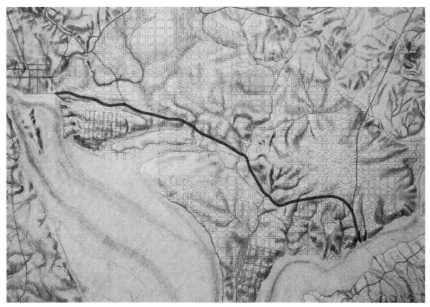

Figure 1 - The Ferry Road

Ferries also came to exist at the foot of South Capitol Street, across at the eastern end of Pennsylvania Avenue and, in 1804, the first bridge at the

Benning farm. Another important north-south trail rose from this same northern shore uphill to the west ultimately to the Forks of the Ohio River.

In the 1790s, Georgetown was already a town with 5,000 inhabitants based upon the port at the mouth of Rock Creek. Moreover, it had grown up at the point where the main north-south road could most easily cross the Potomac River. In 1717, the father of the George Mason of Gunston Hall, one of the drafters of the Virginia Bill of Rights, acquired the island in the Potomac River at the mouth of Rock Creek. Variously known as Mason's Island, Barbadoes Island and Analostan Island, starting in 1748 a highly profitable ferry went from the island, attached by a causeway to the close-by Virginia shore, to the Maryland shore across the wider Georgetown Channel. That was the route taken in April 1755 by General Edward Braddock with his 2100 British regulars from Alexandria on his way west to attack the French Fort Duquesne at the Forks of the Ohio.

This ferry via Analostan Island was replaced by the first bridge across the Potomac upriver at its narrowest at Little Falls in 1797 (now the site of "Chain Bridge"). A ferry had also existed since 1738 at that site where the Potomac River was at its narrowest. A road connected that bridge to Georgetown. The first bridge connecting the Virginia shore directly to the City of Washington was the appropriately named Long Bridge at 14th Street. First built in 1809, it replaced another ferry from the western end of Maryland Avenue. At that time, the far wider expanse of the Potomac River had two separate channels with a sea of mudflats between them. The original bridge thus had draw spans, and sections with partial causeways and piles of rock to hold it all down during periodic ice floes. The original northern channel adjacent to the Washington shore was relatively narrow; there was frequent back-up of water out of Tiber Creek with flooding onto Pennsylvania Avenue by the frozen river.

1.2. The L'Enfant Design

Although a port town already existed, situating the "Seat of Government" at the head of navigation at the confluence of the Potomac River and its Eastern Branch was ultimately an artificial city based on political considerations. Despite the dream of George Washington, a viable commercial city never developed. The Potomac River was not easily converted into a highway of trade to connect the Ohio River Valley to the Atlantic seaboard. The harbor at Georgetown was always overshadowed by deeper water at Alexandria downriver. The canals built in the early 19th century to connect Washington to the Ohio Valley were soon superseded by the Baltimore & Ohio Railroad connecting Baltimore to the west rather than Washington.

The overall design of the City of Washington by Peter L'Enfant was also political in its origins. There was clearly no need for such a large city at that time. The breadth of the city encompassing the entire coastal plain reflected the need to satisfy the Proprietors holding land both to the east and west of Tiber Creek. Its great expanse could also enable the large-scale sale of lots to support the cost of building the large Public Buildings to house the new government. The scale of the city and the costly public buildings also reflected the political vision shared by Federalists such as L'Enfant, Alexander Hamilton and George Washington to have a Seat of Government "worthy of an empire."

The street design imposed upon this grand city was also political in its origins. L'Enfant recognized and capitalized on the existing topography when he placed the "Congress House" on a hill and the "President's House" on a lower knoll one mile away. The one-mile distance separating these hills also can be taken to reflect the sharing of the separate powers expressed in the U.S. Constitution (see Figure 2 for the design by L'Enfant as completed by Andrew Ellicott).

The diagonal avenues are actually pre-eminent to the design; it was the grid that was superimposed. The use of wide avenues connecting the important buildings was to give these buildings prominence. Greatest prominence was given to the "Congress House" reflecting the pre-eminence of the Legislature as Article I in the new Constitution. No less than twenty diagonal streets radiate from the Capitol; at least six were originally proposed to radiate from the "Presidential Palace."

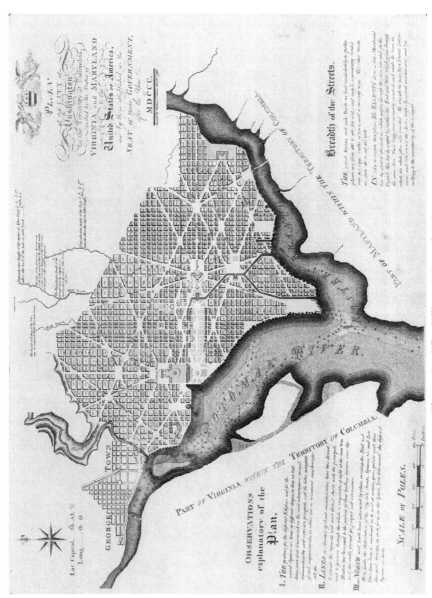

Figure 2 – The Ellicott Map of 1792

4

The greatest of these diagonal avenues connecting the two great public buildings was named after the central state of Pennsylvania. It followed a route separate from the natural one; the east-west "Ferry Road" route was on the ridge connecting the two rivers on a higher land. Pennsylvania Avenue was bound on its southern rim by marshes bordering Tiber Creek. The Central Market placed on the avenue between 7th and 8th Streets NW was known as "Marsh Market." Pennsylvania Avenue flooded frequently until Tiber Creek was roofed over in the 1870s and the Potomac River was dredged starting in the 1880s. Many business establishments originally near the Central Market moved from that area to the higher land along F and G Streets.

Because of its political significance, Pennsylvania Avenue was the one street for which the Federal Government retained responsibility for beautification. Not only used for ceremonial processions such as inaugural parades, Pennsylvania Avenue was also the main street of the Federal City. President Jefferson spoke early of the need for a graveled road from the President's House all the way to the Georgetown Bridge to be eventually in 1822 a western extension of Pennsylvania Avenue.

Pennsylvania Avenue was the street that was paved before all others; first in 1803 during the time of President Thomas Jefferson when gravel was laid and Lombardy poplars planted and in 1821 replaced by sycamore trees along the footways. In 1830, the new Macadamizing process was applied and the original poplars replaced by a variety of trees; and then in the 1870s mainly by maples. In the late 1840s, cobblestones were used; in 1871 wooden blocks; and finally soon after paved with asphalt. In the 1840s, oil lamps lit the street, the only one in the city; in the 1850s, gas lights were used; electricity came in the 1880s.

With the Capitol the focal point, the avenues imposed by L'Enfant on the design other than Pennsylvania Avenue continue to reflect not only the importance of that state but the geography of the country. For example, the more northerly of the states such as Rhode Island and New Hampshire were to the north of the U.S. Capitol. The northern state of Massachusetts, highly significant in the American Revolution, received the name of a northern road particularly important in the street scheme. The name of Virginia, the most important Southern state, was given to one of the more significant roads on that side of the Capitol. Similarly, the names of the Middle Atlantic States such as Maryland and New Jersey were applied to roads emanating from near the center of the Capitol itself. The rest of the street system designed as a grid consisted of numbered north-south and alphabetized east-west streets based on the Capitol. The entire City of Washington was divided into quadrants, again based on the Capitol. Every aspect of the design reflected the role of the city as a political center that mirrored the country and its Constitution.

L'Enfant envisaged the major business street of the country to be the street running east from the Capitol to the Anacostia River. The Capitol faced east in accordance with the orientation to the rising sun. At its mid-point on the way to the Anacostia River, East Capitol Street was to have the stone from which all distances would be measured. Such an arbitrary geometric design failed to materialize on the eastern part of the city. Aside from boarding houses serving to accommodate the members of Congress during their short sessions, the population did not cluster around the U.S. Capitol. Separated by forest and swamp, the Navy Yard adjacent to the river did provide employment; a cluster of houses appeared with its own Eastern Market.

The main growth of the early Federal City moved west toward Georgetown. By 1822, Pennsylvania Avenue entered the President's Park and passed in front of the White House, now bounding the south of the "President's Square". Portions of the ancient east-west "Ferry Road" connecting the two branches of the Potomac formed H Street, thus framing the President's Square on the north. Stephen Decatur had already built his mansion designed by Benjamin Henry Latrobe at the northwest corner; Saint John's Church, also built by Latrobe in 1816, was at the corner of 16th and H Streets. Previously called "President's Park," either James Monroe or John Quincy Adams named the area "Lafayette Square" in honor of the 1824 visit of Lafayette (later altered to Lafayette Park).

In 1850, President Millard Fillmore hired Andrew Jackson Downing to redesign the landscape of Lafayette Park. This was done to receive in 1853 the equestrian statue of Andrew Jackson as well as gaslights and an ornamental iron fence. Clark Mills cast this equestrian statue, the first in the United States. Pennsylvania Avenue continues to Georgetown with a statue of George Washington at the Battle of Princeton in early 1777 in the center of Washington Circle at 23rd Street. Congress commissioned this statue, the first equestrian statue of George Washington, once again by the sculptor Clark Mills. Placed in 1860, it was only the third equestrian statue cast in the United States.

L'Enfant made another major contribution to the design with the use of the projected equestrian statue of George Washington. This was to provide an additional central focal point to unite the two great public buildings. It was deemed so highly important to occasion a visit to America by France's greatest sculptor Jean-Baptiste Houdon to model its subject from life. L'Enfant envisaged the connecting road as a site for embassies and other grand buildings. The term "Mall" was first applied to this potential road by

Andrew Ellicott in his 1792 revision of the L'Enfant Plan. The name derives from a croquet-like game whose French name was Anglicized in the time of Charles II to "Pall Mall," still the name of a street in London where the game had once been played.

Prior to 1850, the Mall area was a large unimproved common area. The "Washington Canal" along the northern edge incorporating the former Tiber Creek was mainly used for the dumping of sewage and garbage from the Central Market. 1847 saw the start of the Smithsonian Castle on the south less marshy side of the Mall, the U.S. Botanic Garden at the foot of Capitol Hill and the Washington Monument at the west end. Andrew Jackson Downing, America's first landscape architect, developed an overall plan that emphasized winding paths and scattered trees eventually implemented between 7th and 12th Streets centered on the Smithsonian Castle.

In the 1850s, the War Department built an Armory for the District of Columbia on the Mall at the present site of the National Air and Space Museum. It became the important extensive Armory Hospital during the Civil War. It received the most seriously wounded since it was the closest to the 7th Street SW wharves where the wounded were landed from the Virginia battlefields; it was there Walt Whitman carried out his "sympathetic visitations." The rest of the Mall was used for military purposes including training of soldiers and the storing and slaughtering of cattle. With the placement of the newly established Department of Agriculture on the Mall in 1868 came attached its more formal garden. Finally, after many temporary usages coincident with the wars of the 20th century, the present-day green lawn was established in accordance with the McMillan Plan of the turn of the 20th century.

1.3 The Transportation System

There had been fords across Rock Creek at what are now P Street and M Street. The latter was usable only at low tide and in good weather so that the need for a bridge was quite evident. The first of the series of bridges connecting Georgetown and the Federal City at the mouth of Rock Creek in 1788 predated the origins of the Federal City. In 1800, a daily stage coach ran between Georgetown and the Navy Yard; the two major settlements utilizing the bridge across Rock Creek at present-day M Street. Bridge Street was the original name for M Street in recognition of this usage. In 1800, a drawbridge was built reflecting the continuing use of Rock Creek by ocean going ships. Soil runoff soon ended Rock Creek as a navigable stream and a covered bridge lasted from 1830s onward. In 1871, an iron truss bridge was built. The present day three span concrete bridge set on beams was built in 1929.

The section of Pennsylvania Avenue between the U.S. Capitol and the White House was the main street of wartime Washington during the Civil War. Prior to the war, there was no more than an urban stagecoach, a horse-drawn omnibus that struggled through the dust and mud of the Washington streets. The first horse drawn rail line was established in 1862 when tracks were finally laid on Pennsylvania Avenue. The horse-cars used the new technology of side bearing rail that could be laid flush with the street surface.

The first line chartered by Congress was the Washington & Georgetown Railroad Company (W&G) to run via Pennsylvania Avenue from Bridge (M Street) and High Streets (Wisconsin Avenue after 1905) in Georgetown to the Washington Navy Yard. The line also connected with the B&O Train Station at the foot of Capitol Hill at New Jersey Avenue and C Streets. Lines also ran north along the 7th and 14th Street corridors to the Boundary Road (after 1890 Florida Avenue). The term referred to the boundary between the City of Washington on the coastal plain and the hillier remainder of the District of Columbia. The Seventh Street line also extended south to the steamboat wharves on the Potomac. Organized initially by Henry Cooke, the brother of the financier Jay Cooke, it was immediately highly profitable based on a fare of 5 cents with free transfers. By 1863, there were 86 cars and nearly 500 horses.

The W&G line was the most famous in the country. It passed the Capitol, the White House, the Treasury as well as the Center Market. By encompassing the Ceremonial Mile on Pennsylvania Avenue, its tracks would line the routes of the parades on Pennsylvania Avenue from the time of the Second Lincoln Inauguration and the Grand Review of the Union armies in 1865 to the Kennedy Inauguration in 1960.

An additional east-west line starting in 1864 was that of the "Metropolitan Railroad Company." As a condition of its charter, unlike its predecessor, it was forbidden to discriminate against Negro passengers from its start. It ran more northerly along H Street to 14th and then along F Street to 5th and then along D Street eventually to New Jersey Avenue and A Street near the B&O station. This became the heart of the later "Washington and Electric Railway" line in the early 20th century. The accompanying figure shows the development of the horse drawn street railways in use prior to the development of electrification. The horse cars

8

were ordered replaced by electric streetcars by 1892. By 1924, there were electric streetcars servicing the entire city and the Virginia suburbs.

The extensive street system laid out by L'Enfant on the coastal plain in the 1790s mainly sufficed through the generation following the Civil War. The subsequent expansion of the City of Washington into the remainder of the District of Columbia with the use of the electrified railways emphasized the importance of the north-south arterial streets. The spine of the major street on the west starts uphill at the Georgetown waterfront. It received its name as "High Street" for its direction to the heights above the town. It rises up the hill to Mount Alban and, as "Tenleytown Road", continues to that crossroad. It branches off there to the west to Great Falls of the Potomac via River Road and north via the Rockville Pike (present-day Rte 355) eventually to Frederick Maryland. The original Georgetown to Tenleytown road received its present name of "Wisconsin Avenue" in 1905 when the electric streetcars began to obliterate differences between areas of settlement and made them integral to the street system of the District as a whole.

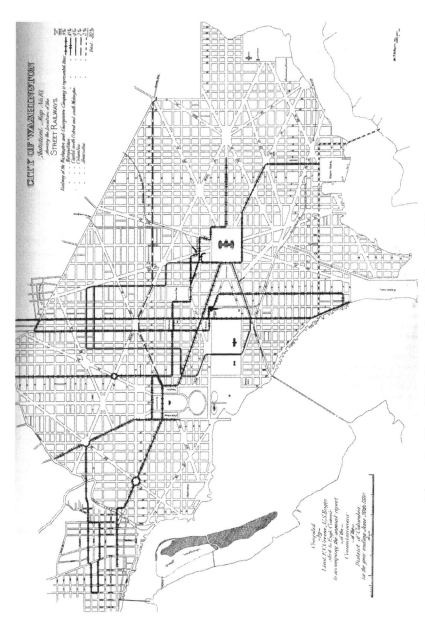

Figure 3 - City of Washington Street Railways 1880

The road to Frederick became more important when in the 1820s it formed the southwestern link of the first "National Road" that extended to Wheeling on the Ohio River, thence all the way to Vandalia in Illinois. Beyond the District Line, the road branches off at Bethesda at what is still called "Old Georgetown Road" on its way west to Frederick while the road directly north went to the county seat at Montgomery Court House (Rockville). One of twelve, a Madonna of the Trail statue stands just prior to that intersection honoring the women who passed through in their Conestoga wagons to settle the "Northwest Territory."

Early horse car lines in the 1860s could not easily ascend what became called Wisconsin Avenue in the west. That area remained undeveloped aside from gentlemen's estates designed as summer residences to take advantage of the cooler elevation. However, the horse drawn cars were able to ascend the less steep 14th Street hill in the east to the early suburbs of Mount Pleasant and Columbia Heights. In the 1890s, electric trolleys surmounted the steeper areas along present day Wisconsin Avenue and the parallel Connecticut Avenue along which suburban development also soon occurred.

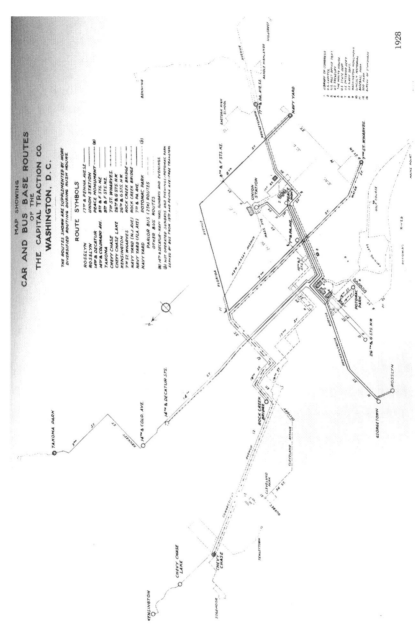

Figure 4 - Capital Traction Lines

12

"The Capital Traction Company" was organized in 1895 as the merger of the original "Washington and Georgetown Railway" (W&G) with the "Rock Creek Railway Company." The latter was organized in 1888 by Francis Newland's Chevy Chase Land Company. It crossed Rock Creek via the Calvert Street Bridge to service his Connecticut Avenue land developments. Starting just east of 7th and U Streets, the "Rock Creek Line" ran along U Street to 18th Street; then up 18th Street before going across a metal bridge at Calvert Street (now replaced by the Duke Ellington Bridge) to reach Connecticut Avenue. Going north along Connecticut Avenue, the line ran across Klingle Valley on another iron bridge (now replaced by the art-deco Klingle Valley Bridge) into Cleveland Park, north to the Chevy Chase Lake, and eventually to Kensington.

"The Metropolitan Railway Company" originally founded in 1864 to run horse cars on H and F Streets, had an extension south to D Street and Indiana Avenue at Judiciary Square. A branch was established in 1868 to run north-south along Connecticut Avenue through DuPont Circle to Boundary Road (Florida Avenue). Another later line in the 1870s entered Georgetown from DuPont Circle over the P Street Bridge; still another line ran along 7th Street Road that became Georgia Avenue, called the "Brightwood Railway".

When first electrified, these streetcars used "trolleys" attached to overhead wires; and then, within the boundaries of the original city of Washington changed to underground electrical conduits via "plows" to avoid the unsightly wires. Electrical conduits were buried between the tracks. The system required each streetcar to use a plow through a slot to reach the source of power. In winter, snow and ice would block the slots; in summer, they would swell. It was rare for there to be a day without problems.

CHAPTER 2
THE DISTRICT OF COLUMBIA

2.1 The Early Suburbs

Washington's population almost tripled during the Civil War from approximately 50,000 in 1860 to nearly 150,000 in 1870. The countryside's rolling hills differed from that of the original city on the coastal plain. During the subsequent process of extension of population into the District of Columbia, the street system laid out by developers did not necessarily conform to the grid pattern laid out by L'Enfant for the original City of Washington.

There were various reasons for such "mis-fit" subdivisions. The first planned subdivision in the District of Columbia was "Uniontown" laid out in 1854 to provide housing in Anacostia for white Navy Yard workers across the 11th Street Bridge. A compact 17-block town site, it was a dense grid that fully used the small amount of flat land available along the river shore without seeking to align their town with the grid of the city of Washington. The District's next subdivision immediately after the Civil War was the open ground "Barry Farm" between Uniontown and St Elizabeths Hospital. The one-acre lots were designed not only as home sites but to include gardens that enabled the newly freed to be self-sufficient. In recognition of the cost of imposing a grid on the rolling landscape, a meandering road system used the existing rural roads to the extent possible.

Unlike working class whites or newly freed blacks, the "LeDroit Park" subdivision sought a wealthy white clientele. Immediately north of Boundary Road (Florida Avenue) between 2nd and 7th Streets, its streets were deliberately laid out at an angle to those streets south of Boundary Road. Entry gates existed at 2nd and 7th Streets to prevent admittance to non-residents. The mainly detached houses were high-priced. At the terminus of the 7th Street horse car line in the 1870s, it was to be a fashionable "romantic" suburb with about 50 Italianate "picturesque" villas designed by James McGill in the style of Andrew Jackson Downing. The author of Cottage Residences in 1842 and Architecture of Country Houses in 1850, Downing was America's first landscape architect responsible for the "romantic" design of the National Mall adjacent to the Smithsonian Castle and that of Lafayette Park near the White House.

The name of the subdivision was derived from LeDroit Langston, a successful real estate agent, whose son and son-in-law were the developers. The 55 acre subdivision was a triangle five blocks wide and 4 blocks deep. What later became 2nd Street was called LeDroit Avenue; all other streets both north-south and east-west were named after trees. For example, what became 3rd Street was called Harewood, 4th Street was called Linden, 5th Street was called Larch and 6th Street was called Juniper. The east-west Streets were Maple (later T Street), Spruce (later U Street) and Elm followed by Oak.

Created in 1870, immediately north of LeDroit Park was "Howard town," It eventually ran from V Street to Bryant Street between 2nd and 5th Streets. Blacks were able to live there. During the 1880s, the "LeDroiters" recurrently erected fences dividing the two subdivisions to exclude inhabitants of Howard town. The 'Fence war" raged through most of the 1880s. In 1886, the LeDroit Park property owners initially petitioned the DC Commissioner for their streets to become connected to the existing grid and the removal of the fence to enable through traffic.

In 1893, the first Black person bought a house in LeDroit Park. Other Black residents followed. The period of racial integration was short lived; by 1900 it had became entirely Black as whites moved to the newly opened suburbs even farther north. Living near Howard University and the Black business center that arose at 7th and U streets, its elite black professional inhabitants during the next generation of segregation were a roll call of the community's leading physicians, ministers and educators. For example, Paul Lawrence Dunbar, the Negro poet, lived there for a short time at the turn of the century.

The other early suburban development was the suburb of "Mount Pleasant," a name reflecting the bucolic character of a plateau between the valleys of Rock Creek and its Piney Branch. It was at the apex of the 14th Street hill, also called Meridian Hill for the early meridian that ran from the White House. Also attached was the name of "Columbia Heights" that reflected the existence on that same hill of the "Columbian College in the District of Columbia" (the predecessor of present day George Washington University).

Originally granted in the 17th century by Lord Baltimore to James Holmead, the entire tract was then called "Pleasant Plains." Holmead Place still remains in recognition of the original owner. During the early part of the 19th century, a race track owned by John Tayloe occupied much of its flat area to the north.

The very top of the hill was originally part of a farm called "Mount Pleasant" owned by the Peter family, prominent merchants in Georgetown. A portion of that land was sold in 1811 to Commodore David Porter. Born in Boston in 1780, Porter had fought the Barbary Coast pirates. Wealthy because of prize money, Porter built a house astride the meridian line he called "Meridian Hill."

At the time of the Civil War, the Colombian College, founded in 1821, occupied a house on the hill adjacent to the Porter home that was commandeered by the Union forces protecting the city. The Porter home was one of several in the area used as a hospital until it burned in 1863. Other military hospitals in the area included the 800-bed Columbian College Hospital, the 1300-bed Carver Hospital and, close by on 14th Street, the 1600-bed Mount Pleasant Hospital.

The land owned by the "Columbian College in the District of Columbia" in the area of Meridian Hill received the name of College Hill and then Columbia Heights. When the nearby east-west streets were cut through, Chapin, the name of an early president of the college, remained on the map of the District of Columbia as did Columbia Road, the name of the college and Euclid as the great geometer. Other nearby streets such as Harvard, Kenyon and Princeton continued the academic theme.

In 1850, a major portion of the 73 acre tract to the west bordering Rock Creek was sold to William Selden, once Treasurer of the United States. A southern sympathizer, in 1862 Selden sold the land to Samuel P. Brown. After use during the Civil War for a hospital near the present corner of Mount Pleasant and Newton Streets, Brown built a mansion there that he called "Mount Pleasant" In the decades following the Civil War, land adjacent to the Rock Creek Valley was being subdivided. Brown laid out as a subdivision starting in 1865 an area atop Meridian Hill stretching almost from the valley of Rock Creek on the west to 14th Street on the east and from Columbia Road on the south to the valley of the Piney Branch of Rock Creek on the north. He designated this relatively flat plateau as the "Mount Pleasant" subdivision. Its elevation made it more desirable for home sites, less likely to support the breeding of mosquitoes.

In the 1870s, Brown was appointed to the Board of Public Works in the Territorial Government. It was no accident that Mount Pleasant's streets were then macadamized and kept open year round "making it one of the finest suburban drives close to the city." This new subdivision with lots no smaller than one acre attracted government clerks, mainly from New England that formed a fine community. However, streets in this village were laid out haphazardly and at angles not in conformity to the earlier grid pattern in the city as designed by L'Enfant.

14th Street on the eastern edge of the subdivision was the main arterial street with a small shopping area at 14th and Park Road (then Peirce Mill Road). Brown and his associates laid out new streets parallel to Park Road (now Lamont, Monroe, Newton and Meridian Place) following to some degree the contours of the land but also their boundary line. There were few streets that crossed at right angles and none that connected to existing streets in the city. Still recalling the so-called "misfit subdivisions," the street pattern extending west from 14th Street persists to this day not in conformity with the strictly rectangular pattern elsewhere.

Starting in the 1870s, a horse car ran on the relatively easy hill on 14th Street from Boundary Road (Florida Avenue after 1890) but many persons walked to their government offices. The "walking-horse car " era ended when the electric streetcar 14th Street line reached Mount Pleasant in the 1890s from the streetcar line already on Pennsylvania Avenue. The competing Metropolitan Railway, whose ownership conveniently included Samuel P. Brown, entered Mount Pleasant from the west to Park Road and 14th Street via Columbia Road from Connecticut Avenue in 1903.

Sixteenth Street, originally projected to extend to the District Line as "Meridian Avenue" in a comprehensive 1887 plan, was finally driven in 1901 through the old Mount Pleasant neighborhood. A wide street of relatively stately buildings, it separated east from west. The name of the less fashionable "Columbia Heights," given earlier to the easterly area between 11th and 13th streets in honor of the old college, became attached to the area along 14th Street.

The "Mount Pleasant" name was attached to the area west of Mount Pleasant Street. (Old 16th Street). Increased development occurred to the west. Still extant neo-Georgian mansions appeared on Park Road; row houses began to appear on the other streets that had been brought into conformity with the grid pattern by the Highway Act finally passed in 1893. The western edge abutting Rock Creek was an estate called Ingleside. Originally, the home of Henry Ingle, a friend of George Washington, the mansion was owned between 1850-1890 by the Walbridge family. Their name remains on Walbridge Terrace on land they subdivided following the Highway Act. After having been the "Ingleside Presbyterian Home," the mansion remains the "Stoddard Baptist Home" in the 1800 block of Newton Street. It retains the appearance of an Italian villa imparted by its architect, Thomas U Walter, also the architect of the U.S. Capitol Extension. Even further west was the estate called "Rosemont." The name remains on the bi-lingual pre-school in what was formerly The Episcopal House of Mercy, a home "for wayward girls."

The long-time shopping district at 14th Street and Park Road was embellished in 1922 by one of the first branches of the Riggs Bank modeled with its columns with the Ionic order after its impressive main office across from the Treasury. In 1924, the magnificent Tivoli Theater completed what was, until the era of the automobile, the major shopping area of the east side of the city.

2.2 Creating the "Permanent Highway System"

The sub-divisions created during the 1870s and later had streets that were generally narrower than the corresponding city streets that ranged from 60-90 feet. The status of these streets north of the city limits was described as follows: "some of the north-south numbered streets were laid out as extensions of the city streets; some were not. The diagonal avenues were not generally prolonged. The cross streets were laid out at varying angles. Adjoining subdivisions differed from each other so that a street upon one side would have no extension on its neighbor. "

From the early 1880s, there were plans to extend the system of streets and avenues of the city northward. The principle had been established in 1887 to maintain the existing grid pattern for the extension of existing streets. The law passed by Congress in 1888 required that streets in all new subdivisions be continuous with city streets and of at least 90 feet in width with avenues named after states at 120 feet width. Streets running east-west would be named from the letters of the alphabet as before but for the principal American cities alphabetically; then alphabetically for the principal American rivers and lakes.

However, there was no provision to deal with the streets in the sub-divisions existing prior to the passage of the 1888 law or for determining the costs for bringing about such conformity. In some instances, streets laid out after the 1888 law in conformity with the city streets did not connect with the streets of earlier subdivisions. As late as April 1896, a letter to the *Washington Post* complained that there was still enough uncertainty concerning streets actually to be built in a previously existing subdivision to inhibit land sales.

Another problem remained in the naming of the east-west streets. DC Supreme Court Justice Alexander B. Hagner recommended the entire abolition of the use of alphabet letters for the naming of streets, even those already so named in the City of Washington. To obviate confusion such as on the telephone and in court testimony, he proposed the use of names rather than merely letters. He further proposed that they use names of famous Americans, cabinet members, Supreme Court Justices and even mayors of Washington, all without regard to the number of syllables. Indeed, ultimately the selection of many of the bi-syllabic street names of famous Americans were drawn from his list of suggested names.

The naming of streets in Georgetown in conformity with the overall plan took place in 1905. It was at that time that "Reservoir Road" and "Volta Place" as well as "Wisconsin Avenue" got their present names. Only streets retaining their previous names are Potomac, Prospect, Olive and Grace.

Finally, after several modifications, the policy proposed in 1903 was finally implemented in 1905. The first tier of east-west city streets would remain named merely by letters of the alphabet; the second tier after famous Americans in alphabetical order using two syllables, including many of those recommended by Hagner; to be followed by names of American cities and rivers with three syllables.

For example, streets in the northwest quadrant named initially after cities such as "Savannah" became "Sedgwick;" "Vallejo" became "Van Ness"; "Utica" became "Upton," all in the second tier of alphabetized streets. In the third tier of the alphabetized east-west streets, "Albemarle" and "Brandywine" remained but "Des Moines" became "Davenport" (presumably retaining the reference to Iowa) to accord with its presence among the three-syllable tier of names of American places. Similarly, the names of streets east of the Anacostia River were changed in 1908 with Good Hope Road and Alabama Avenue made up of several previously separately named segments. The hilly character of this area led to considerable variation in the street scheme from that of the northwest quadrant and the perpetuation of many of the earlier two-syllable American place names such as "Bangor" and "Camden."

The issue of streets not conforming to the grid pattern arose again when applied to the hilly areas adjacent to the valley of Rock Creek. It had been recognized that modifications would need be made. One such arose in the design of the Cleveland Park sub-division. In the early 1790s, Benjamin Stoddert and Uriah Forrest bought from George Beall the land formerly called the "Rock of Dumbarton, Addition to the Rock of Dumbarton and Beall's Lot." The land ran from the east side of what was laid out as the Road to Tenleytown all the way to the west side of Rock Creek. Called by them "Pretty Prospect," it contained about 860 acres going as far north as present day Melvin Hazen Park beneath the Klingle Road Bridge.

In 1890, the electric streetcar was introduced on the west along Tenleytown Road; and in 1892 to the east on Connecticut Avenue, the latter as part of the development extending to Chevy Chase in Maryland. The area between these two arterial streets became "Cleveland Park" named after Grover Cleveland, the owner of a portion of the original Forrest farm as his residence during his first term. Development of the housing lots in Cleveland Park started in 1895. The first portion of Newark Street was laid out between 33rd Street west to Wisconsin Avenue and Ordway Street from 34th to 36th Street. Some of this had been part of Grover Cleveland's Oak View property, thus its appellation. The streets were laid out in a standard grid pattern consistent with the existing street requirements of the District of Columbia established by the 1893 law.

The Highway Act of 1893 included an appropriation for the planning services of the Olmsted Brothers firm. Frederick Law Olmsted Jr and his half-brother John Charles Olmsted had succeeded Frederick Law Olmsted in the family firm of landscape architects in Brookline Massachusetts. They emphasized the need for streets to conform as much as possible to the existing terrain. They felt that this served to control costs of construction, prevent erosion and provide "a pleasing and picturesque appearance." This philosophy was followed in their work on the design of the Cleveland Park street system in 1895-96. An additional area, "Cleveland Park Addition," east of 33rd Street, contains Highland Place and the rest of Newark Street. This portion followed the contours of the land to a greater degree. The present-day curvilinear design on the streets between Rodman and Newark east of 34th Street is also in accordance with the suggestions of the Olmsted firm in their 1897 Report "Permanent Highway Plan for the District of Columbia."

As other areas were developed, they too were exempted from the requirements of the grid. Another example was a 1910 Special Act of Congress that exempted subdivisions known as "Massachusetts Avenue Heights" and "Massachusetts Avenue Park" encompassing the area north of Massachusetts Avenue abutting Rock Creek Park (now called "The Woodland Drive Normanstone" neighborhood.) The purpose was "to preserve the area's natural beauty, encourage 'widely spaced residential development' and the 'retention of much handsome tree growth', generally bringing about a most attractive park-like result."

.

CHAPTER 3
ROCK CREEK PARK

3.1 Rock Creek

L'Enfant designed the "City of Washington" in the 1790s on the roughly triangular coastal plain between the Potomac River on the south and its Eastern Branch we call the Anacostia. North of its original boundary at Florida Avenue, is an ellipse of low hills forming a natural amphitheater? Rock Creek runs into the Potomac from north to south in a rocky glen through this amphitheater. It marks the boundary between the older harder Piedmont plateau to the west and the softer coastal plain. The headwaters of the creek lie in Montgomery County near Laytonsville 16 miles north of the District line. The stream winds though a rolling countryside until it becomes steeper in the District cutting through rocky narrow ravines until it flattens out south of P Street on its way to the Potomac. A trading post at its mouth eventually became the nucleus of the port of Georgetown first laid out in the 1750s.

The first major landowner in the late 17th century was Henry Darnall whose nearly 1800 acre "Gyrle's Portion" was part of an overall 6000 acre holding. In the 18th century, Daniel Carroll married the Darnall daughter and styled himself "Daniel Carroll of Rock Creek." He was one of the first set of commissioners responsible for completing the original city and the cousin of "Daniel Carroll of Duddington," the largest landowner of the area that became Capitol Hill.

The early history of Rock Creek was focused on its commercial value. The Creek was navigable initially up to P Street but soon silted over. However, during the 19th century, based on its gradient and substantial water flow, a number of mills were established along its course. By 1840, milling of locally raised grain was the largest industry in the District.

Peirce Mill at Tilden Street and Beach Drive N.W. is a reminder of that time. It was an integral part of a diversified farming operation that included the growing of grain and vegetables, a distillery and grist mill. Isaac Peirce, a Quaker, migrated from Chester County near Philadelphia in the 1780s. In recognition of his large land holdings, he was appointed in 1802 by President Jefferson to the Levy Court. It acted as the Board of Commissioners of the County of Washington, the area of the District of Columbia not included in the L'Enfant designed City of Washington.

Figure 5 - Peirce Mill

Peirce expanded his holdings along Rock Creek with the still extant stone mill, built in 1829 of local stone quarried on his property. George Shoemaker, another Quaker of Pennsylvania extraction, married in 1815 Abigail Peirce, the youngest daughter of Isaac Peirce. Their son, Peirce Shoemaker became a Catholic and a Democrat when he married in 1855 Martha Carbery of the slave-holding family of a former Washington mayor. The Peirce-Shoemakers were substantial slaveholders as evidenced by their application for compensation for 32 slaves freed by emancipation in the District of Colombia in April 1862. Peirce Shoemaker remained the largest single private landowner in 1890 when Rock Creek Park was established. The Peirce Mill ceased commercial operation following the 1870s with the large-scale transfer of wheat production and milling to the mid-West. Restored during the 1930s as part of President Franklin Roosevelt's New Deal, it has had a variety of uses since then. Other substantial landowners were Thomas Blagden and Hiram Walbridge whose land became respectively "Crestwood" and "Mount Pleasant." Blagden ran the "Argyle Mill" on the creek and his name lives on in "Blagden Avenue."

Joshua Peirce, another son of Isaac, held the property extending to the west up what he called "Linnean Hill" in honor of the Swedish botanist Linneus. He developed extensive plant nurseries there (now Marjorie Meriwether Post's Hillwood Museum and Garden). He popularized the camellia, imported from China, but also the less desirable English ivy and multiflora rose. His nephew and heir Joshua Peirce Klingle closed the plant nursery and lived in "Cloverdale," still used as the National Park headquarters for Rock Creek Park. He also gave his name to the Klingle Valley of Rock Creek, now the site of the art-deco Klingle Valley Bridge on Connecticut Avenue that marks the southern boundary of Cleveland Park.

Street names such as present day Adams Mill Road reflect ownership by the Adams family of the former Columbia Mill on the lower portion of the Creek. Benjamin Stoddert first placed a mill there on his property of "Pretty Prospect" he had bought with Uriah Forrest. 42.5 acres were sold to Jonathan Shoemaker in 1800 to form the ongoing Columbia Mills property that he operated until 1809. Roger Johnson, the brother of the Maryland Governor Thomas Johnson, rebuilt the mill after a fire in 1812. During his ownership, a house was built, probably during 1809-1818 for use by his second son George Johnson and his family. In the simplified neo-Palladian design of a country villa, its architect is thought by some to be William Thornton. In 1820, the mill operated 5 milling stones grinding wheat, corn and plaster of Paris. Sold by the elder Johnson to John Quincy Adams in 1824, it thus became known as Adams' Mills.

President John Quincy Adams entrusted the mill in 1826 for a time to the unsteady hands of his alcoholic youngest son John until the latter's death in 1834. It was finally sold by the Adams family in 1872 when the mill no longer operated. No remains are visible. Water flow was always uncertain on Rock Creek; the profitable operation of the mills was subject also to the vagaries of the grain market. The house was sold separately from the mill by Johnson family in 1835 to Dr Ashton Alexander and used for a rental property. Dr Henry Holt, a gentleman farmer, bought the house in 1844. Sold to the National Zoological Park, the house, now deteriorating, was kept intact until abandoned as the headquarters of the Zoo in 1988. Other mills on upper Rock Creek live on as Jones Mill Road and Viers Mill Road in Maryland.

During the Civil War, the area surrounding Rock Creek was an integral part of the defensive perimeter. After the disaster of the 1st Battle of Bull Run in July 1861, it became obvious that the rather haphazard defenses built thus far protecting the southern approaches to the city of Washington were insufficient. General McClellan, now in command of the newly constituted Army of the Potomac, designed a ring of 48 forts with 300 cannon. Eventually the forts covered all the stream valleys, roads and railroads that entered Washington from all directions. Given the low water in the Potomac in the fall that made the city vulnerable from the north, major forts on the northern rim were built. Fort DeRussy was immediately west of Rock Creek adjacent to Milk House Ford, Fort Pennsylvania (later Fort Reno with present-day Reno Road), Fort Massachusetts (later Fort Stevens), Fort Totten (still a Metrorail station), and Fort Lincoln (an area still astride the important road to Baltimore and the B&O Railroad). Mainly completed during the winter of 1861-1862, they were extended and reinforced after the 2nd Battle of Bull Run in the summer of 1862 and again in 1863.

By the end of 1863, there were 63 forts, 93 batteries and 837guns along with 25,000 men. Many of the large guns had been made according to the method invented by Thomas Jackson Rodman. The "Rodman gun" he invented exceeded the previous limits of cast-iron cannon and was also a far more reliable and stronger weapon. His new "wet chill" method involved casting around a hollow core while cooling the inside of the barrel. The huge guns he was able to make, as large as 15-inch bore, were primarily used for permanent fixed positions such as the circle of forts protecting Washington.

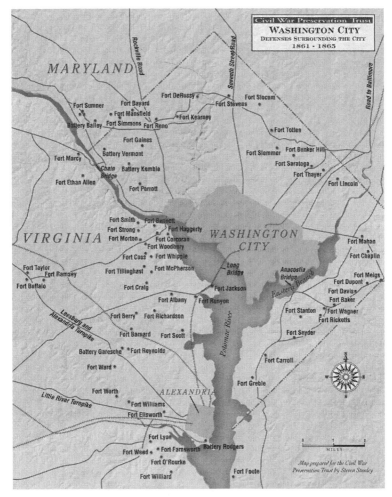

Figure 6 - Ring of Forts: The Defenses of Washington

Cannon peered through the earthwork walls reinforced by logs felled from the surrounding woods. The effect of such felling of trees was long lasting. For example, the heavily forested ridge overlooking the Anacostia River from the east became barren ground that remained permanently denuded. The run off soil after rain required dredging to keep open a channel to the Navy Yard; the Anacostia River never recovered.

The Civil War changed Tenleytown from a sleepy little country crossroads to a military camp as part of the defenses of Washington. Fort Reno was the major fort at the very highest point in the District of Columbia at over 400 feet just north of Tenleytown. Named after the general killed at South Mountain on 14th September 1862 just prior to the

Battle of Antietam, it commanded the Tenleytown Road and the Rockville Pike. A camp of Rhode Island soldiers also existed on River Road just behind the Methodist church on the grounds of the Methodist Cemetery. This is still the site of a church. The strong fortifications at Fort Reno dissuaded the Confederates under General Jubal Early in July 1864 from attacking there; instead, he attacked the less formidable Fort Stevens further east before being driven off.

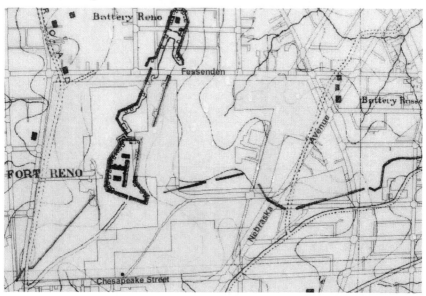

Figure 7 - Fort Reno

The presence of the Union soldiers in Tenleytown attracted free blacks and "contraband" slaves and was the forerunner of an integrated community, called Reno City that existed until the mid-20th century adjoining the site of the fort. It was mainly obliterated in the 1930s in favor of the playing fields of the newly constructed Woodrow Wilson High School. The Jesse Reno School for Colored Children, built in 1903-04, located adjacent to the Alice Deal Middle School, is a reminder of Reno City's existence.

The present day "Military Road" crossing the tip of Rock Creek Park is north of the actual squigglier military road built in the fall of 1862 that connected the forts along the northern perimeter. It ran from near Chain Bridge on the west to Fort Stevens at Georgia Avenue to service the chain of forts defending Washington from attack. The Civil War military road also connected with the newly cut "Grant Road" at Tenleytown. This rather meandering street still contains some of the early frame houses that characterized the Tenleytown neighborhood in the 19th century.

3.2 The McMillan Commission

Officially known as the "Park Improvement Commission for the District of Columbia," the McMillan Commission arose in the context of the centennial in 1900 of Washington as the United States capital. A Washington architect and historian, Glenn Brown had become Secretary of the American Institute of Architects (AIA) in 1898. Brown had studied the work of Peter L'Enfant and actively advocated the revitalization of Washington's central core based upon L'Enfant's designs. Brown was also inspired by the Columbian Exposition of 1893 as a model of what might be achieved in Washington. As the son of an Alexandria physician interested in the high incidence of waterborne disease, Brown was also cognizant of the threat to public health of the sewers of Georgetown and Northwest Washington emptying into Rock Creek. There had been proposals to encase in a tunnel the waters of Rock Creek from O Street to Pennsylvania Avenue with roads built on the landfill connecting the city and Georgetown over the tunnel.

Glenn Brown had also been involved with the group that had been instrumental in achieving the passage of the law establishing Rock Creek Park. He had worked, in conjunction with the Olmsted landscaping firm, in the design of some of the early animal enclosures at the Zoo to reflect the natural habitats of the various species. For example, he designed an Asian-inspired Zebu House. Brown also used natural boulders in the design of the footbridges that were a model for those later recommended for Rock Creek Park by the Olmsted firm. Brown's most lasting contribution to the embellishment of the Rock Creek Valley was the 1915 "Dunbarton Bridge" with its buffalo sculpture crossing from Georgetown to Q Street that became a model for subsequent bridges crossing Rock Creek.

Brown was remarkably well-connected based upon his classmates at Washington and Lee and later at M.I.T. His writings in 1896-1897 on the history of the U.S. Capitol and its architect William Thornton brought him to the attention of Senator James McMillan, the Michigan Republican who was Chair of the highly important Senate District Committee. Glenn Brown planned a symposium on "The Federal Buildings and Their Grouping" to take place at the AIA convention in Washington in December 1900 in conjunction with the celebration of the centennial of the Capital. There were several aims: one was to bring to the attention of Congress the value of designing massing of landscape, buildings, and sculpture (in the style of the Columbian Exposition); another was to emphasize the importance of establishing a commission of experts to consider the various suggestions afoot for the celebration of the centennial. Still another was to wrest control of improvements of federal buildings from the U.S. Corps of Engineers. As an example, Brown particularly attacked the plan offered by Colonel Bingham of the U.S. Corps of Engineers for increasing the size of the White House "as a violation of its character." The goal was to insure that such future efforts would be entrusted to professional members of AIA.

Immediately following the AIA convention, Senator McMillan insured the publication of its proceedings as a Senate document and initiated the formation in March 1901 under Senate auspices of "a commission …who shall [have as its] subject the location and grouping of public buildings and monuments to be erected in the District of Columbia and the development and improvement of the entire park system of the said District." Daniel Burnham, the leader in the building of the Columbian Exposition along the Lake Michigan shoreline of Chicago was the first invited. Frederick Law Olmsted Jr. was also among the first appointed, to take the place that had been held by his now ailing father on the original Exposition. They in turn invited the architect Charles Follen McKim, the leading American architect, partner in the firm of McKim, Mead and White and, still later, Augustus Saint-Gaudens, the leading American sculptor. Both had also been associated with the Chicago Fair.

Figure 8 - The Court of Honor of the Columbian Exposition of 1893

Frederick Law Olmsted Jr. would make his first substantial mark on the city of Washington through his participation on the McMillan Commission; the youngest member of this auspicious body, Olmsted was a key contributor to the ideas and outcomes that emerged from this planning. He was the primary author for the parts of the Commission Report that dealt with the park-related concerns. The larger part of the Report dealt with these park recommendations with extraordinary sensitivity to the natural attributes and recreational requirements of the region. As a counterpoint to the formally treated areas of the government center, Olmsted, in a manner worthy of his father, promoted a park system of naturalistic design.

A major theme was a network of public open spaces with interconnecting parkways– a system encompassing the entire District of Columbia and extending to the region. The focus in Northwest Washington was the importance of maintaining the natural character of Rock Creek Park and a parkway to Georgetown connecting the Rock Creek Park to the projected development of West Potomac Park. It was no mere happenstance that Olmsted remained intimately involved with the ongoing development of Washington's major urban park. The influence of his father's ideas, his own educational development, and his ultimate perceptions about city planning all made him an appropriate candidate to plan this important public resource. Olmsted would assume that role more emphatically with a 1918 report which laid out a more detailed plan for the park and his subsequent work with the National Capital Park and Planning Commission (NCPPC).

In 1910, a Commission of Fine Arts (CFA) was established under President William Howard Taft to further implementation of the Report of the original McMillan Commission. It was successful in fulfilling many of the recommendations of the Commission in respect to the Lincoln Memorial and the development of the Federal Triangle. The connecting Rock Creek Parkway became the major "park" recommendation that was implemented in the early years of the CFA.

Olmsted himself was able to guide its development and to maintain an open Rock Creek from P Street south rather than its encasement in a tunnel. In June 1910, he was appointed as one of the first group of members of the CFA. He was appointed vice-chairman after death of Burnham in 1912 and reappointed in 1914 by the Democratic President Wilson to serve until 1918.

3.3 Rock Creek Park

The valley embracing Rock Creek had long been appreciated for its natural beauty and variety, but its importance grew as the capital city expanded after the Civil War. There was enhanced concern about the potential for pollution and an increased desire to preserve land as settlement expanded. There was also a growing awareness of Washington's status in relationship to other international capitals. For example, an article in the *Evening Star*, then Washington's leading newspaper, spoke to the value of such a park, indicating that while the city had developed in many ways, "when we come to the matter of that indispensible feature of a first-class city, a great public park supplying a health and pleasure resort for all classes, the comparison of Washington to the European capitals of London, Paris, Berlin, and Vienna, with their thousands of acres of parks is most humiliating."

The establishment of the Rock Creek Valley as a park in 1890 coincided with an increased interest in the concept of "national parks" to preserve natural frequently wild landscapes. Located in a valley running north and south from the city limits to the Potomac River, Rock Creek Park contains 1,900 acres, including a 200-acre zoo. Bordered on the east by 16th Street and on the west by Oregon Avenue, from the National Zoo north to the District Line, it divides the somewhat separate street systems of the District of Columbia east and west of the park.

First proposed by General Nathaniel Michler in 1867, the park was accomplished under Charles Glover, president of the Riggs Bank, and Crosby Noyes, editor of the *Washington Evening Star* and members of the newly re-established Washington Board of Trade. After the establishment of the National Zoological Park in 1889, legislation was finally enacted in September 1890 authorizing the creation of its contiguous "Rock Creek Park." A Board of Control led by members of the U.S. Army Corps of Engineers was appointed to manage the park.

The only early major improvement of Rock Creek Park itself had been an extensive road system along the east side of the creek built under the direction of Captain Lansing Beach, the Engineer District Commissioner after 1898. In 1916, a proposal was submitted to the Control Board governing Rock Creek Park for a playground and recreation area near the Brightwood Reservoir adjoining Sixteenth Street in the area of the present-day Fitzgerald Tennis Stadium. This caused alarm about the heretofore haphazard development and the need for a well-developed plan. In May 1917, the Olmsted Brothers firm of landscape architects was formally commissioned to prepare a report on the improvement of Rock Creek Park.

In his interim report, Olmsted affirmed his essential approach to landscape design: "The essential justification for this large park is unquestionably found in the recreation value of its wild or "undeveloped" qualities—large stretches of natural forest, river valleys, rolling hills, and occasional meadow lands—and use of exploitation or development of any sort can never be right that is not based upon that fundamental conception." This understanding of the role of the landscape architect puts him at the service of the landscape rather than in domination of it. Olmsted also reiterated his father's theme of the social benefit of the park: "No matter how perfect the scenery of the Park may be or may become, no matter how high its potential value, that value remains potential except insofar as it is enjoyed by large and ever larger numbers of people, poor and rich alike."

The core of the final Olmsted Report on Rock Creek Park focused on the key principles of land preservation and restoration of the scenery without the introduction of foreign elements, the opening of the park to the public in a way that would not detract from its essential park-like qualities and adequate roads and other transportation to provide access to and through the park. The plan delineated the various existing natural segments of the park that would enable a variety of uses. Olmsted's plan has in large part been sustained, despite the evolving nature of recreation in America. Paved roads that now carry automobile commuters have replaced dirt carriageways. Nonetheless, the park still serves the city as an escape from the hard surfaces of the metropolitan landscape. In accordance with the principles of the Olmsted Report, the bridges spanning Rock Creek within the Park have also been designed to be subordinate to nature.

Figure 9 - Bridge in Rock Creek Park

With development of Northwest Washington and Montgomery County, sewer lines were built diverting many of the streams and tributaries feeding into Rock Creek and reducing its flow. It was necessary to have a regional planning agency to preserve the stream flow and prevent pollution of Rock

Creek. In June 1924, Congress created a National Capital Park Commission (NCPC). The act authorized the commission "to acquire such lands within the District of Columbia and adjoining areas in Maryland or Virginia as were necessary for the proper and comprehensive development of the park, parkways and playground system of the National Capital."

By 1925, significant tracts were purchased including the area known as Klingle Valley, an important access to Rock Creek Park from the west, and the gift of Glover-Archbold Park, providing a connecting link from the Foundry Run Valley to the Rock Creek Valley. In April 1926, there was a broadening of the composition of the commission and a change in name to the National Capital Park and Planning Commission (NCPPC). The original officers were joined by four presidentially appointed citizens. It was at this time that Frederick Law Olmsted Jr was named to the commission. Now in his own right a figure of long professional experience nationwide and having lines of communication with influential people, Olmsted made substantive contributions to the Planning Commission, contributing to the park-like quality of the Washington area that has made it the envy of other American cities.

SECTION II
THE NAMES OF THE STREETS

INTRODUCTION

The principle of the north-south streets numbered from their distance from the U.S. Capitol in the various quadrants could be maintained in general as the population spilled into the entire District of Columbia. The Highway Plan established by the successive Acts of 1888 and 1893 seemed to answer that need. The extension of the earlier avenues named after the original states; and avenues named after the other additional states was similarly implemented. The latter was carried out, but somewhat less systematically than heretofore, in replicating the geography of the country. What was particularly problematic was the continuation of the principle of the lettered east-west streets as the population extended northward all the way to the District Line at a distance from the U.S. Capitol.

The principle was reinforced that the national capital should reflect the country. The decision was also to maintain the principle of lettered streets in alphabetical order. However, the basis for the choice of their names and the need to reflect the distance from the U.S. Capitol in some systematic fashion was resolved only after some delay. Ultimately, most particularly west of the Anacostia River, the second tier of streets would reflect mainly the bi-syllabic names of famous Americans; the third tier would reflect as before the names of American places, but also conform to the use of tri-syllabic words. The choice of sometimes somewhat obscure "famous Americans," augmented by military leaders, conformed largely to that offered by Alexander Hagner

There are a few bi-syllabic names of places that remain that intrude into the scheme of "famous Americans" such as "Newark" and "Quebec." There are also a few tri-syllabic famous Americans such as "Garrison" and "Harrison" that intrude upon the alphabetical list of American places that form the majority of the third tier place names. The presence of Rock Creek Park provided a natural division that was also translated into the different nomenclature for the two sides of the District. Streets not part of the rectangular plan are designated "Place," Court" and rarely "Road" when useful to do so. The over-riding consideration could be met that no two streets would bear entirely the same identification.

The names of these east-west streets are listed in this section in alphabetical order in the categories of most numerous "political figures" and "military figures" and then the less numerous "other scientific and artistic figures."

34

CHAPTER 4
AMERICAN POLITICAL AND MILITARY FIGURES

4.1 American Political Leaders

There are somewhat over seventy names, some rather obscure, of various members of the Congress and cabinet members along with each of the presidents of the 19th century. The selection of additional names essentially ended when the street names were definitively established in 1905. They are listed in alphabetical order.

There is but one Adams Street although there is an Adams Mill Road and an Adams Court and Adams Place. The Adams family produced two presidents.

Born in Massachusetts, **John Adams** was an important figure in the American Revolution, Minister to London and vice-president before becoming the second president in 1797. A Federalist, he was the last president of his party overturned by the Jeffersonian Democratic-Republican Party in the election of 1800. However, the Federalist idea of the enhanced role of the central government vis a vis that of the states reappeared later in the 19th century in the guise of the program of the Whig party and then in the Republican party. Adams is most remembered for having moved the Continental Congress to issue the Declaration of Independence in 1776.

John Quincy Adams, the son of John Adams and the sixth president from 1825 to 1829, is also recognized obliquely as the owner of an early mill on lower Rock Creek by Adams' Mill Road. Secretary of State under President James Monroe, he is credited with the issuance of the "Monroe Doctrine." He was elected president in a controversial vote in the House of Representatives in 1824 after failing to receive a majority in the Electoral College. Andrew Jackson felt that he had been deprived of the presidency despite having achieved a plurality in the popular vote. He accused Adams of a "corrupt bargain" for having appointed Henry Clay, former Speaker of the House, as Secretary of State, considered the stepping stone to the presidency. Adams is unique in becoming a long-time member of the House of Representatives after having been president. He was a strong abolitionist and was instrumental in preserving the legacy of James Smithson to create the Smithsonian Institution.

William B Allison was born in Ohio in 1829, educated at Wooster Academy and graduated from Western Reserve College in 1844. He eventually moved in 1857 to Dubuque Iowa where he practiced law. He was elected to the U.S. Congress in 1862 and remained in the U.S. Senate from 1872 until his death in 1908. Because of his seniority, he chaired the Senate Committee on Appropriations and other important committees. He is best known for his sponsorship of the Bland-Allison Act of 1878 that increased the use of silver for coinage despite the veto by President Rutherford Hayes.

Adelbert Ames was born in 1835 in Rockland Maine. He graduated from West Point in 1861 and served in the U.S. Artillery, eventually winning a Medal of Honor for his actions at 1st Battle of Bull Run in July 1861. He then served in the Peninsular Campaign, winning a commendation and promotion at the Battle of Malvern Hill. In command of the 20th Maine Volunteer Regiment, he then rose to brigade and then division commander for the Battle of Gettysburg where that regiment famously defended Cemetery Hill on the 2nd July. Transferred to the South, he led his division at Fort Fisher during the capture of the port of Wilmington North Carolina in early January 1865.

During the era of "Congressional" Reconstruction, he was appointed Military Governor of Mississippi and later elected Republican Governor and then U.S. Senator for Mississippi in 1870 by the newly enfranchised Blacks. His marriage to the daughter of Benjamin Butler brought him riches in the post-Reconstruction era.

Francis Asbury was born in 1745 in Staffordshire England. Raised from infancy for the ministry, he was appointed at age 22 as a preacher by John Wesley. A missionary to America, he was appointed in 1784 one of the first bishops of the Methodist Episcopal Church in the USA. Preaching everywhere a crowd would gather, by the time of his death, the number of Methodists had reached several hundred thousand.

Edward D. Baker was born in London England in 1811 of poor Quaker parents. The family immigrated to Philadelphia, then to New Harmony Indiana the utopian community of Robert Owen and finally to the Illinois Territory. Baker eventually read law and became an intimate friend of Abraham Lincoln. Fellow Whigs in Springfield, the two men alternated in running for Congress from Illinois. With the demise of the Whig Party, Baker entered politics as a Free-Soiler when he moved to California after 1850. He eventually was elected Oregon's Republican senator in 1860.

He served to introduce his friend Lincoln to the audience prior to the president's inaugural address in March 1861. Due to his military background in the Mexican War, Baker was appointed colonel and, despite the need to retain his key senatorial seat, commander of a brigade in the division of General Charles Stone. Abraham Lincoln was very visibly moved when his close long standing friend Baker was killed in action at the Battle of Balls Bluff in October 1861.

Joseph K. Barnes was born in Pennsylvania in 1817 and eventually graduated from the University Of Pennsylvania Medical School in 1838. He was a surgeon first in the U.S. Navy, then in the U.S Army in the Seminole Campaigns and in the Mexican War. A protégé of Secretary of War Stanton, he replaced Surgeon General William Hammond in 1863 while continuing some of the innovations in ambulance service and field hospitals already instituted for the Medical Department of the Union army. Still Surgeon General, he cared for Lincoln and Seward in April 1865 and then in the care of President Garfield at the time of his assassination in 1881.

Edward Bates was born in 1793 on the family plantation in Goochland County Virginia. After service in the War of 1812, he moved to St Louis where he read law. At various times after 1822 he was a member of the Missouri legislature. In the 1840s, he was a prominent Whig in association with Henry Clay. Now a Republican, he was an unsuccessful candidate for the Republican 1860 presidential nomination. Appointed by President Lincoln as Attorney-General in 1861, he resigned in 1864 in opposition to the issuance of the Emancipation Proclamation and the recruitment of Black soldiers to the Union army.

Lansing S. Beach was the Army officer assigned responsibility in 1899 for the maintenance and building of roadways in the newly established Rock Creek Park. His name was given to the still important road he had built along the east bank of Rock Creek.

James G. Birney was born in 1792 in Danville Kentucky. He graduated from Princeton College in 1810 and studied law in Philadelphia. Although from a slave holding family, he opposed slavery. He became in 1823 an officer of the American Colonization Society to encourage the removal of freed slaves to Liberia. Moving to Cincinnati, he founded in 1836 an abolitionist paper The Philanthropist that advocated a "moderate" discussion of slavery. Nevertheless, it became the object of attacks culminating in the destruction of his printing press in the July 1836 "Cincinnati Riot." In 1837, Birney became an officer of William Lloyd Garrison's more radically abolitionist American Anti-Slavery Society and the presidential candidate of the anti-slavery Liberty Party in 1840 and 1844.

James G. Blaine was born in 1830 in Pennsylvania. He entered Pennsylvania's Washington College in 1843, and then taught at Georgetown College in Kentucky where he met his future wife, a native of Maine. They moved to Kennebec and later Portland Maine where he owned newspapers. Active in Maine Republican Party state politics, he was elected to Congress in 1862 as a strong supporter of the Union. He remained in Congress, becoming Speaker from the 41st through 43rd Congresses (1869- 1874). He was the leader of the so-called "Half-Breed" branch of the Republican Party that moved the party to the support of industrialization and the high tariff away from its other roots supporting the abolition of slavery.

By now a member of the Senate, favored at the start of 1876 Republican Convention, he lost the nomination to Rutherford Hayes; again favored in 1880, he lost it to James Garfield due to the undying personal enmity of New York Senator Roscoe Conkling and rumors of a scandal involving the Union Pacific Railroad. President Garfield appointed him Secretary of State but Garfield's death in 1881 led to Blaine's resignation from the cabinet of the successor President Chester Arthur, a protégé of the inimical Senator Conkling.

Finally nominated for president in 1884, Blaine lost to Grover Cleveland when the reform wing of the Republican Party defected. Reappointed Secretary of State by President Benjamin Harrison in 1889, Blaine was able to carry out some of his aborted earlier initiatives by convening in 1890 the Conference of Pan-American States, the forerunner of the present-day Organization of American States (OAS).

Francis P. Blair was born in 1791 in Abington Virginia. Moving to Kentucky, he graduated from Transylvania College in Lexington Kentucky in 1811. He came to Washington in 1830 in the train of President Andrew Jackson to found the Washington Globe and the Congressional Globe. Although a Democrat, he was opposed to the extension of slavery to the territory gained during the Mexican War. He supported in 1848 Martin Van Buren as the candidate of the Free-Soil Party and then in 1856 John Fremont of the Republican Party. A close adviser to President Lincoln, he advocated an active role to sustain Fort Sumter in April 1861. His son Montgomery Blair was Postmaster General and a conservative voice in the Lincoln cabinet until his resignation in 1864.

Sayles J. Bowen, born in New York in 1813, moved to Washington in 1835. An active abolitionist, he supported the Free Soil candidacy of Martin Van Buren and was one of the founders of the Republican Party. He was elected mayor of Washington in 1868 with the large support of the newly franchised freed Blacks. His term was marked by the first large expenditures for colored schools and public works that gave work to his supporters. He was defeated in the election of 1870 that led to the Territorial form of government for the District of Colombia.

Robert Brent (of Brentwood) was born in 1764 in Stafford County Virginia. His mother was a member of the eminent Catholic Carroll family. He married Mary Young whose father Notley Young was one of the largest landowners in the new Federal City. His family quarry in Virginia was the source of the sandstone used in the building of the White House and U.S. Capitol. With the establishment of the municipal government, President

Thomas Jefferson appointed him the first mayor. Serving successive terms until 1812, Brent established the entire range of municipal services. In 1817, he presented to his daughter Eleanor as a marriage present the estate of Brentwood with the house designed by Benjamin Henry Latrobe

William J. Bryan was born in 1860 in Salem Illinois to a religious family. His own conversion at age 14 he deemed central to his own life. He saw his Christian religious commitment also central to his political commitment to the "Social Gospel." He graduated from Illinois College in 1881 and then law school in Chicago. In 1887, he moved to Lincoln Nebraska and became noted in the 1890s for his oratory in favor of "free silver." The unsuccessful candidate for president when nominated in 1896, the previously more conservative Democratic Party incorporated his agrarian Populist agenda for debt relief against the "gold standard" of the Republican Party. Once again the unsuccessful Democratic Party candidate in 1900, he also opposed imperialism after the Spanish-American War as inconsistent with American principles of "rule with the consent of the governed." Bryan did least well in 1908 for his third run against William Howard Taft.

In recognition of Bryan's constituency within the Democratic Party, President Woodrow Wilson appointed him Secretary of State in 1913. Opposed to intervention in the European war, he resigned in 1915 following Wilson's harsh speech after the sinking of the Lusitania by German submarines. After World War I, he helped pass the 18th Prohibition Amendment and spoke of the dangers of Darwinian evolution. Dying soon after, he represented the "World Christian Fundamentals Association" in the prosecution of the Tennessee teacher of Darwinism in the famous 1925 "Scopes Trial" when Clarence Darrow was the opposing lawyer.

James Buchanan, the 15th president from 1857 to 1861, was born in Franklin County Pennsylvania in 1809 and grew up in Mercersburg. He graduated from Dickinson College in Carlisle Pennsylvania in 1809. He practiced law in Lancaster and ran as a Federalist for state office. Now a Democrat, he served in Congress from 1821-1831; then in the U.S. Senate from 1834-1845. As Secretary of State under President James K. Polk, he negotiated the Oregon Treaty delineating that boundary with British Canada. Minister to Court of St James from 1853-1856, he was nominated for president based on his distance from the sectional battles in the Congress dealing with the admission of Kansas to the Union.

This issue persisted and grew larger despite his efforts during his presidency to support the pro-slavery forces in Kansas. The Supreme Court's "Dred Scott" decision in 1857 further exacerbated the sectional rivalry that led to the break-up of the Democratic Party; the election of the

Republican Abraham Lincoln; the subsequent secession of the Southern states and Civil War.

Charles Carroll was the recurrent name of several generations of the senior branch of this leading Maryland Catholic family. The original Charles Carroll was the founder of the line in the New World when he immigrated to St Mary's City in the 17th century. His son styled as "of Annapolis," was in turn the father of the Charles Carroll "of Carrollton." Born in 1737, this last was educated in Europe at the Jesuit College of St Omer and St Louis-le-Grand. One of the richest landowners in the colonies, he opposed the British imposition of taxes. As the delegate of his colony to the Continental Congress, he was the only Catholic signer of the Declaration of Independence.

Daniel Carroll was the name of several members of this leading Maryland Catholic family in the early days of Washington. One styled as Daniel Carroll "of Rock Creek" was one of the first Commissioners appointed to oversee the development of the site for the Seat of Government. Another styled as Daniel Carroll "of Duddington" was one of the largest landowners of the eastern portion of the new District. One of L'Enfant's less politic actions was to remove the house the well-connected Carroll had started to build astride the projected New Jersey Avenue. The name of that house lives on with the street that still remains on Capitol Hill.

George Calvert was the family name of the 1st Lord Baltimore, the proprietor of the colony of Maryland. Born on the family estate in Yorkshire, he was raised as a hidden Catholic forced to swear conformity to the Protestant faith. George Calvert trained at Trinity College at Oxford and studied law at Lincoln's Inn. Closely allied to very influential Sir Robert Cecil, Calvert rose to power and wealth with the accession of James VI of Scotland to the English throne as James I. Calvert finally declared his Catholic faith in 1625 and resigned his offices. He provided a sanctuary for English Catholics in the New World, first at "Avalon" in Newfoundland; and then in more temperate Maryland. His son, Cecilius, was the first governor of the latter colony. Leonard Calvert, his grandson, was in turn the founder of the first settlement at St Mary's City in 1642.

Simon Cameron was born in 1799 in Maytown Pennsylvania. Apprenticed to a printer, he became an editor in Harrisburg in 1824. He organized the Northern Central Railroad allied with the Pennsylvania Railroad in the 1840s. First a Whig, then a Democrat and, finally a Republican in 1856, he was elected to the U.S. Senate representing the needs for a protective tariff by the Pennsylvania ironmasters. A candidate in 1860 for the Republican presidential nomination, his switch to Abraham Lincoln brought him an appointment as Secretary of War in 1861. Charges of corruption caused his resignation in January 1862 to be replaced by Edwin Stanton. Back in the Senate in 1866, he remained until 1877 after assurance that his son James Donald Cameron would be his successor.

Salmon P. Chase was born in 1808 in Cornish New Hampshire. After the early death of his father, he was raised under the care of an uncle Episcopal Bishop Philander Chase; He graduated from Dartmouth College in 1826 and moved to Cincinnati after studying law. He became involved with the anti-slavery movement when he came to the aid of James G. Birney during the Cincinnati Riot of 1836. In association with such others like Harriet Beecher Stowe, he helped found the anti-slavery Liberty Party in Ohio. Merged into the Free Soil Party, he was elected U.S. Senator in 1849 where he served as the voice of the anti-slavery movement in opposition to the Compromise of 1850 and the Kansas-Nebraska Bill.

One of the founders of the Republican Party, he was the first Republican Governor of Ohio. A leading contender for the Republican presidential nomination in 1860, he was appointed Secretary of the Treasury by President Lincoln in 1861. He helped manage the financing of the war by printing greenbacks, selling bonds with the aid of Jay Cooke and raising an income tax for the first time via the Internal Revenue Service. President Lincoln accepted his oft-proffered resignation in 1864 but soon after appointed him Chief Justice of the Supreme Court to replace Roger Taney. In that role, he officiated at the impeachment trial of President Andrew Johnson.

Henry Clay was born in 1777 on the family plantation in Hanover County Virginia. He was raised in Richmond Virginia where he read law in the office of George Wythe, Jefferson's mentor. In 1797, Clay moved to Lexington Kentucky. His estate there called "Ashland" had 600 acres and up to 60 slaves. Elected to Congress in 1811, he was immediately elected Speaker and remained so during his six following terms. He led the so-called "War Hawk" faction in the House in favor of the War of 1812 and supported the Tariff of 1816 designed to protect manufactures but also to raise money for internal improvements. This"American System" for internal infrastructure improvements that he advocated was similar to the Federalist spirit of the "American Plan" of Alexander Hamilton.

He negotiated the Missouri Compromise of 1820 to deal with the extension of slavery into the land acquired by the Louisiana Purchase. It defined the northern boundary of Arkansas below which slavery was permitted (with the exception of Missouri itself as a slave state), and the entry of Maine as a free state to maintain the balance in the Senate.

With Clay's support, **John Quincy Adams** was chosen as president in 1824 when he won the majority of the votes in the House of

Representatives. Clay was accused of a "corrupt bargain" by the Jacksonians when he was appointed Secretary of State. Now in the Senate after 1833, Clay negotiated an end to the "Nullification" crisis when South Carolina threatened to secede over the Tariff of 1828 that raised duties to the benefit of Northern manufacturers. The leader of the newly named Whig Party, he then organized in 1832 opposition to President Jackson's actions concerning the Second Bank of the United States.

Clay was unsuccessful in gaining the Whig presidential nomination in 1840 in favor of the war hero William Henry Harrison; although nominated in 1844, he lost to James Polk. Clay lost the nomination in 1848 to still another war hero Zachary Taylor. Once again back in the Senate, Clay proposed a set of amendments to deal with the extension of slavery into the lands acquired from Mexico. Unable to carry the vote for what was called the Compromise of 1850, he retired to enable Stephen Douglas to do so.

Grover Cleveland was born in 1837 in Caldwell New Jersey where his father was the Presbyterian minister. Due to his father's transfers, Cleveland lived in various New York towns before finally moving to Buffalo in 1853. Having studied law, he practiced there as well as entering local Democratic Party politics. During the Civil War, he evaded conscription by hiring a substitute. Elected reform mayor of Buffalo in 1882, he became Governor of New York in 1884. Aided by the defection of the reform wing of the Republican Party, Cleveland defeated a ticket led by James Blaine and John A Logan. The first Democratic president since James Buchanan, Cleveland followed the traditional Democratic Party stance on lowered tariffs but also supported hard money and limiting pensions of Union veterans. He was defeated in 1888 by the Republican Benjamin Harrison, partly based on his veto of the Pension Bill sponsored by the GAR (Grand Army of the Republic).

The nominee of the Democratic Party once again in 1892, his vice-president was Adlai Stevenson of Illinois. The latter, a "silverite," served to balance the ticket. The Panic of 1893 led to labor unrest. Cleveland used federal troops to break the Pullman Company strike that had been aided by the American Railway Union led by Eugene V. Debs. A non-interventionist, he refused to support the annexation of Hawaii after the overthrow of the native rulers by American interests. His name remains on the sub-division of Cleveland Park that was the site of his home during his first term after his marriage to the young Frances Folsom.

George Clinton was born in New York in 1739. Active in Ulster County New York politics, he was a member of the New York Colonial Assembly and successively re-elected Governor of New York from 1777 to 1792. An Anti-Federalist, he opposed John Adams for vice-president in 1792, was elected vice-president along with Thomas Jefferson in 1804 and with James Madison in 1808. He remained favored as a presidential candidate by those opposed to James Madison, but died in March of 1812. His nephew DeWitt Clinton became famous as promoter of the Erie Canal.

John J Crittenden was born in 1787 near Versailles in central Kentucky, the border slave holding state with which he was identified throughout his long life. He studied at the College of William & Mary, practiced law in Louisville, and finally, starting in 1819, in the Kentucky state capital of Frankfort. His political career was strongly identified with that of Henry Clay and the Whig Party in opposition to Presidents Andrew Jackson and Martin Van Buren. He was a member of the U.S. Senate on several separate occasions interrupted by service as Attorney General in the cabinets under both Whig President William Henry Harrison (John Tyler) and President Millard Fillmore.

Once again, in the U.S. Senate in the 1850s, he opposed secession and founded the Constitutional Union Party that nominated John Bell in the election of 1860. It won majorities in several of the Border States but did not affect the election of Abraham Lincoln. After the election, Crittenden offered a set of constitutional amendments in the "Crittenden Compromise" designed to prevent secession by meeting in large part the demands of the South. This effort foundered on the unalterable stand of Lincoln not to accept any further extension of slavery as the bedrock of the Republican platform. Crittenden then helped insure that Kentucky did not secede from the Union and returned to Congress to represent his state in the 37th Congress.

Jefferson Davis was born in 1808 in Kentucky, attended Transylvania University in Lexington Kentucky before graduating from West Point in 1828. He left the army to become a cotton planter in Warren County Mississippi. His first wife, the daughter of General Zachary Taylor, died of malaria soon after their marriage. He remarried Varina Howell in 1845. He commanded a volunteer Mississippi regiment during the Mexican War, famous for his action at the Battle of Buena Vista in February 1847 under his erstwhile father-in-law.

A U.S. Senator from 1847, he resigned to run unsuccessfully for governor of Mississippi but was then appointed Secretary of War under President Franklin Pierce in 1853. After 1857, he was again a U.S Senator until the secession of his state. Although personally opposed to secession, he was a leading spokesman for states rights and the slavery interest. Elected president of the Confederate States of America (CSA), he was inaugurated at Montgomery Alabama on February 18th 1861.

His role during the Civil War was made difficult due to his own ill health and psychological frailty. Moreover, he was forced to seek centralized power to fight a war for survival when the country he led was fundamentally based on states rights. Limited by the actions of the increasingly hostile Confederate Congress, he also found generals such as Joseph E Johnston recalcitrant to direction. Robert E Lee was more compatible but the overall success of his Army of Northern Virginia could not alone maintain the CSA against the overwhelming military and economic superiority of the Union.

Noted for his role on the Confederate side during the Civil War, the appearance of his name on the streets of the Union capital of Washington DC presumably reflects membership in the cabinet as Secretary of War between 1853 to 1857 as well as his bravery in the Mexican War.

Samuel Dexter was born in Boston Massachusetts in 1761, graduated from Harvard College in 1781 and read law in Worcester with Levi Lincoln, later Attorney General. He entered the 3rd Congress and then, as a Federalist, the U.S. Senate. For a short time in 1800 he was Secretary of War under President John Adams, He later joined the anti-Federalists in support of the War of 1812.

John A. Dix was born in 1798 in Boscawen New Hampshire. He served in the U.S Army until 1828 rising to the rank of captain. He moved to Cooperstown New York to manage the extensive land holdings of his wife's father. Active in New York state politics, he was Democratic U.S. Senator from 1845 to 1849 and unsuccessful Free Soil candidate for New York Governor defeated by the Whig Hamilton Fish. Defeated by the Whig William Seward for the U.S. Senate, he was Secretary of the Treasury under President James Buchanan. He became one of the heroes of the North known for his adamant stand against the take over of the U.S. Treasury stores in New Orleans at the start of the Civil War.

Appointed a general in the New York militia, he was instrumental in maintaining Maryland within the Union during the early days of the Civil War. Connected with Thomas Durant, he was president of the Missouri and Mississippi Railroad in the 1850s and the Union Pacific in the 1860s.

Stephen A Douglas, born in Vermont in 1813, moved to Illinois in 1833 and considered himself a westerner. Married to a southerner, his political ambitions profited from her inheritance that included a cotton plantation with its slaves. A U.S. Representative from Illinois and then its Democratic Senator, by virtue of his oratory and legislative skills, he was the Senate's dominant figure in the 1850s. As Chair of the Committee on Territories, he was instrumental in the passage of the bills that created the Compromise of 1850 that appeared to settle the issue of the extension of slavery. However, his Kansas-Nebraska Bill of 1854 based on "popular sovereignty" reopened that question and led to the formation of the Republican Party. Despite his success in the senatorial election of 1858, the Lincoln-Douglas debates of that contest brought Lincoln to national prominence. Douglas was the unsuccessful presidential candidate of the northern branch of the Democratic Party in 1860 when Lincoln was elected.

Frederick Douglass was born in 1818 to a slave mother on a plantation in Talbot County Maryland. He was initially taught to read against the law forbidding such education for slaves by a compassionate white woman and was able to learn about politics. This experience of power through education became one of his basic ideas. Another came from achieving manliness by his fighting back against a cruel master who tried to break him by beating him. Finally escaping to freedom in 1838, he became a spokesman for both abolition and women's rights achieving support in Europe as well as in the North. Editor of *The North Star* in Rochester New York, he then moved to Washington in 1872 to become editor of *The New National Era*, a weekly newspaper devoted to increasing Black participation in American life.

The life and career of Frederick Douglass in Washington reflected the opportunities that Reconstruction offered and its limitations. His life story as a former slave on Maryland's Eastern Shore had great value in achieving support for emancipation. He had enormous faith in the effects of the 13th Amendment abolishing slavery but only as the first step. Civil Rights appeared to be guaranteed by the 14th Amendment in 1868. He looked further. Voting Rights were still not guaranteed until the 15th Amendment was ratified by 1870. He still thought a major deficiency was that no effort at land distribution ever succeeded at providing economic opportunities to the former slaves.

Douglass was initially supportive of the Territorial Government for the District of Columbia starting in 1870. Although concerned about the dilution in Negro voting power, he approved since it apparently applied to both races. He was for a short time appointed to the Territorial Upper House. He retired in favor of the appointment of one of his sons. All District voting rights were abolished in 1874 by the end of the Territorial Government. Moreover, the election of President **Rutherford Hayes** in 1877 was part of a bargain that ended Reconstruction in the South. As if in partial recompense, Douglass received from Hayes in 1877 his first federal appointment as the not inconsequential positions as U.S. Marshall of the District of Columbia and then later Recorder of Deeds.

As his political power waned, Douglass in his personal life carried on as a representative of Negro emancipation but now in terms of being a respectable property owner. He owned two houses at 310-318 A Street N.E. on Capitol Hill (later the temporary site of the Museum of African Art) that he had joined together to provide a home for his children. They were in the Second Empire Mansard style prevalent in the still fashionable 1870s Capitol Hill. In 1877, Douglass also bought a property he called "Cedar Hill" from Uniontown's bankrupt segregationist developer thus ending the exclusion of Negroes. The message of the last decades of his life when segregation was intensified was to fight back by accumulating property and leading an integrated personal life. The image he presented was as a man of letters and property owner.

The Cedar Hill estate (now a National Historic Site) was thus an important part of his life and career as a pioneer in Negro rights. The white pillared house with a verandah on a hill is part of the message. Like the plantation on which he had been born in a slave cabin, he created on his property a garden and woodland. The "big house" in which he lived counters the previously despised maternal black side of his ancestry. He built his study as a man of letters what could have been a small slave cabin on the property. He invoked the cedars on the property as similar to those near the slave cabin of his grandmother with whom he had lived and brought soil from there to Cedar Hill to nourish the trees.

The furnishings of the interior also project an image consistent with his message. The West Parlor of Cedar Hill has a picture depicting Othello confidently and comfortably telling his life story, the scene that Shakespeare alludes to in his play as leading Desdemona to fall in love with him. The room also includes a miniature copy of *The Greek Slave* by Hiram Powers, so often used as an icon by abolitionists. Pictures and heirlooms are displayed as though of his abolitionist "family." These include among others both Wendell Phillips the white abolitionist and Blanche K. Bruce, the black Senator from Mississippi elected in 1878. The East Parlor has a table formerly owned by abolitionist Senator Charles Sumner and a rocker given him when Douglass was Minister to Haiti. Finally, a picture at Cedar Hill shows him from behind at work at his desk surrounded by books. The bridge that bears his name runs as an extension of South Capitol Street to the South East quadrant of the city with which he was identified.

John Eaton was born in Halifax County North Carolina in 1790. Moving to Tennessee, he became in 1818 U.S. Senator intermittently until 1829 when he entered the cabinet as Secretary of War of his close friend President Andrew Jackson. His second wife Peggy O'Neil Timberlake was shunned for her lowly origins by the ladies of the other cabinet members led by the wife of John C. Calhoun. The angry President Jackson caused the resignation of the entire cabinet to the advantage of the career of the then bachelor Martin Van Buren, The latter replaced Calhoun as vice-president in Andrew Jackson's second term and went on to the presidency in 1829.

George F. Edmunds was born in 1828 in Richmond Vermont. After studying law, he became a member of the Vermont House and then its upper chamber before entering the U.S. Senate in 1866. During his long career ending in 1891, he was chair of a number of Senate committees, candidate for nomination at the Republican presidential conventions of 1880 and 1884 and an author of the Sherman Anti-Trust Act of 1890.

William M. Evarts, born in Boston in 1818, was the grandson of Roger Sherman, one of the signers of the Declaration of Independence. A graduate of the Boston Latin School, Yale and Harvard Law School, his law career was mainly in New York. A Whig before becoming a Republican, he nominated William Seward for president at the 1860 convention. A respected lawyer, he was Chief Counsel for Andrew Johnson at his 1867 trial for impeachment, then Republican counsel on the 1877 Electoral Commission that selected Rutherford Hayes as the successful presidential candidate. He was Secretary of State in the cabinet of President Rutherford Hayes. Active in opposition to the corrupt ring led by Senator Conkling at the New York Custom House, he became U.S. Senator from New York from 1885 to 1891. Active also in international affairs, he was most noteworthy for leading the American effort for the pedestal for the Statue of Liberty, unveiled in New York Harbor in 1886.

William P. Fessenden was born in 1806 in New Hampshire but lived mainly in Maine. He graduated from Bowdoin College in 1823, studied law and practiced mostly in Portland. The son of an anti-slavery activist, he served in the Maine legislature before being elected as a Whig to Congress for the first time in 1840, to the Senate in 1854 as a Whig and in 1860 as a Republican. Head of the Senate Finance Committee, he was associated with Secretary of the Treasury Salmon Chase in methods for financing the war. He succeeded Chase as Secretary of the Treasury in July 1864 and was successful in financing the remainder of the war by issuing bonds with Jay Cooke rather than printing greenbacks. Returning to the Senate, he headed the Joint Committee on Reconstruction. A "moderate," he voted against conviction of President Andrew Johnson during the trial for impeachment.

Millard Fillmore, the 13th president, was born in Cayuga New York in 1800. He struggled to obtain an education in this frontier area and eventually read law. Settling in the Buffalo area, he was elected as a Whig to Congress from 1832 to 1843; was chosen as vice presidential candidate and presided over the Senate during the debates leading to the Compromise of 1850, which he later supported. He also supported the implementation of the controversial Fugitive Slave Act after he succeeded President Zachary

Taylor after the latter's death in 1850. Fillmore was responsible for having Andrew Jackson Downing carry out the design of Lafayette Park to receive the equestrian statue of Andrew Jackson. In foreign affairs, he initiated the excursion led by Matthew Perry to open up Japan to western trade although finally accomplished during the following Pierce administration. The presidential candidate of American Party (Know-Nothing) in the election of 1856, he helped assure the election of the Democrat James Buchanan. Fillmore's most noteworthy effort was devoted to the founding and early development of the University of Buffalo.

James A Garfield, the 20th president, was born in northeastern Ohio in 1831 as the youngest of five. Raised by his widowed mother, he struggled to achieve an education. Educated first at what became Hiram College, he also later taught there after graduating from Williams College in 1856. Opposed to slavery, he commanded a Union regiment and then became chief-of-staff to General Rosecrans in the Army of the Cumberland at the Battle of Chickamauga. Elected to Congress in 1862, he remained a key member until elected Senator in 1880. Instead of assuming that office, Garfield became the Republican nominee for president chosen as the result of a deadlocked convention. His term was cut short after only 200 days, dying in mid-September after being shot on 2nd July 1881 by a deranged office seeker. His major initiative for civil service reform was accomplished by his successor Chester A Arthur in 1883.

William L. Garrison was born in 1805 in Newburyport Massachusetts. Apprenticed to a printer, he became a newspaper editor. Converted to anti-slavery views in 1828, he later became editor in Boston of *The Liberator*, the leading anti-slavery newspaper. The founder of the American Anti-Slavery Society, he advocated women's suffrage and temperance along with unequivocal abolition of slavery. Supportive of the Union during the Civil War, he maintained his commitment to abolition until its achievement 1865 with the passage of the 13th Amendment.

Ulysses Grant was born in 1822 and raised in Ohio. The eighth generation of an American line traced back to Connecticut in 1630, he was born in a small town in Ohio across the river from Kentucky. An ambitious newly prosperous farmer and tanner, his father's decision to move from Kentucky to the free state of Ohio is credited to antipathy to the sale of slaves.

Graduating in only the middle of his class from West Point in 1843, Grant was assigned to the infantry rather than the cavalry that he had wished and for which he was well-suited. Grant was a quartermaster on the Texas border in an infantry brigade assigned to protect the artillery of **George Thomas** on the march to Monterrey during the Mexican War. While in the army after the war, he was separated from his family on a lonely assignment on the Pacific coast and acquired a reputation as an alcoholic. After resignation from the army and his return to Missouri, he failed at a number of jobs and ended in May 1860 as a clerk in his father's store in Galena, Illinois.

In the spring of 1861, in the fever of widespread enlistment, Grant was appointed colonel and commander of a volunteer regiment. He would never actually lead a regiment in combat; by August 1861, he was appointed a brigade commander and a general. From the start, Grant showed the characteristics that differentiated him from other commanders. As a former quartermaster, he was concerned with procuring the supplies needed for his troops. When they were not forthcoming from the ordinary army channels, he would try other ways by resourcefulness and brute force. He would not idly sit by nor complain of inadequate supplies to justify inaction. He was also aided in Washington in his career by his politically potent mentor Illinois Republican Congressman Elihu Washburn, a close friend of President Lincoln.

In February 1862, Grant captured Fort Henry at the mouth of the Tennessee River. With the conquest of Fort Donelson at the nearby mouth of the Cumberland River, he acquired the nickname of Unconditional Surrender Grant. The major battle at Shiloh Church (Pittsburg Landing) on April 6 1862 found Grant unprepared for the attack. After two days of bitter fighting, the Confederates retreated. Both sides falsely claimed victory but the heavy toll of Union dead or wounded could not be explained away. General Henry Halleck, jealous of Grant's successes and thinking little of him because of his low rank at West Point, temporarily deprived Grant of command of the Army of the Tennessee.

Once Halleck was called to Washington to function as general-in-chief., Grant was able to show his skill in pursuing single mindedly the strategic goal of opening up the Mississippi River. His victory at Vicksburg in July 1863 was a model of long range persistent planning. Grant had also learned after Shiloh that the destruction of the Confederacy would require the destruction not only of its armies but the sources of its supplies. The destruction of resources became an end beyond merely the requisition of necessary supplies. In his devotion to "total war," he also welcomed the feasibility of using the freed slaves as combatants.

Grant was now overall commander in the west with George Thomas the commander of the Army of the Cumberland. Unexpectedly, the Army of the Cumberland captured the heights of Missionary Ridge overlooking Chattanooga. The victory at Chattanooga in November 1863 and later the capture of Knoxville confirmed Grant in March 1864 to be the general-in-chief Lincoln had been seeking. Grant agreed to carry out a coordinated campaign in both theaters and to destroy the Confederate armies rather than merely gain territory.

With 50,000 casualties during the six weeks Overland Campaign in the spring of 1864, Grant had still not destroyed the Army of Northern Virginia. However, the 32,000 casualties suffered by Lee's army could not be as easily made up. Making frontal assaults on the entrenched Confederates was finally called off after Cold Harbor just twelve miles from Richmond. The race then began on June 12 to reach Petersburg where the railroads converged that fed Richmond. The capture of Petersburg would lead to that of Richmond and did so in the spring of 1865 with surrender of Lee's army at Appomattox.

General Grant became closely involved with the struggle between President Andrew Johnson and the Congress over Reconstruction. Elected in 1866, the veto-proof Republican majority 40th Congress passed a new Reconstruction Bill. The former Confederate state governments recently established under the lenient rules defined by President Andrew Johnson were subject to review. Military commanders would be in control until each state framed a constitution guaranteeing equal legal and political rights to all its citizens, including those newly freed. Already, a bill had been passed that the Army Commanding General (Grant) could not be removed without the consent of the Senate. The military governors of the former Confederate states were thus subject to General Grant, more trustworthy to follow the Congressional dictates, rather than President Andrew Johnson as commander-in-chief.

To prevent removal of the thousands of Republican office holders by a president who had in fact Democratic Party roots, a "Tenure of Office Act" had been passed by the 40th Congress. That Act served also to protect **Edwin Stanton** as Secretary of War, sympathetic as he was to the radical Republican Congressional cause. For example, Secretary Stanton had acted in support of General **Phillip Sheridan** in his conflict with the former rebels in Louisiana's provisional government. With Congress once again adjourned, President Johnson dismissed Stanton in July 1867 and also acted to remove General Sheridan in favor of General Winfield Scott Hancock, more sympathetic to the South. Despite the refusal of Stanton to resign, Johnson appointed General Grant as interim secretary of war. Grant, having accepted the appointment as secretary of war, nonetheless opposed the president's action in recalling Sheridan. President Johnson's attempt to force Stanton's departure from his cabinet became the most important particular of the Bill of Impeachment issued by the House Judiciary Committee in November 1867.

General Grant's stance re Stanton stood him in good stead with the radical Congressional Republicans. Coupled with his wartime record, he was assured the Republican nomination and the electoral victory as the 18th president in 1868. He generally supported Reconstruction but to a lessening degree. His re-election to a second term in 1872 was successful although threatened by the defection of the "Liberal Republicans" under Horace Greeley. They opposed the corruption described as "Grantism" but also favored amnesty for Confederates. With Reconstruction under siege, during 1873-1875 the Negro vote was suppressed and Republican office-holders driven from office by the Democratic Party "Redeemers" in all but three of the formerly Confederate states. Despite several attempts, the history of corruption and scandal made it ultimately impossible for Grant to receive nomination for a subsequent run for office before his death in 1885.

Hannibal Hamlin was born in Paris Maine in 1809. After training at Hebron Academy, he studied law and practiced in Bangor Maine. After a series of state offices, he was elected for several terms to Congress in the 1840s and then to the U.S. Senate in 1848. In opposition to the extension of slavery, he joined the Republican Party in 1856. He balanced the ticket geographically when elected vice-president in 1860 along with Abraham Lincoln. He had little influence during Lincoln's first term and was dropped in favor of the War Democrat Andrew Johnson for the "National Union" ticket in the election of 1864. Hamlin returned to the Senate in 1868 to serve for two more terms.

Alexander Hamilton was born in Nevis in the British Leeward Islands, most probably in 1755. He grew up in St Croix in the Danish Virgin Islands. An illegitimate child, he was orphaned by the death of his mother at age thirteen. Impressed by his writings, community leaders sponsored his migration in 1772 to the mainland to enter King's College in New York (predecessor of Columbia College). Volunteering at the start of the American Revolution in 1775, he was made captain of artillery and fought at the Battle of White Plains and at Trenton in 1776. He then became lieutenant-colonel and aide to General **George Washington**. A close personal relationship developed in which Washington trusted him with a wide range of important duties. Still intent on establishing a record of military glory, Hamilton resigned his position with Washington so that he could take an active combat role at the Battle of Yorktown in 1781.

In recognition of the problems faced by the Continental Congress's lack of finances, Hamilton advocated a central government stronger than the Confederation; less dependent on the states and able to levy independent taxes. Although he found the results of the 1787 Philadelphia Constitutional Convention still wanting, he campaigned actively for its ratification in the *Federalist Papers*. He was appointed by President Washington to be the first secretary of the treasury in 1789. During his tenure, he saw his role to be a leader in the development of a strong executive and of a system for public credit including a national bank. He issued a series of Reports during 1790-1791 outlining these plans and fought to have them implemented.

Secretary of State **Thomas Jefferson** led the opposition in the cabinet; James Madison led the opposition in the Congress with the eventual formation of the anti-Federalist Democratic-Republican Party. Hamilton supported the 1794 Jay Treaty favorable to Great Britain and the Quasi-War against France during 1798-1799, both opposed by the Jeffersonian party. Hamilton was killed in 1804 in a duel with Aaron Burr over a feud based on New York politics.

Benjamin Harrison, the grandson of William Henry Harrison, was the 23rd president from 1889 to 1893. A veteran of the Civil War and a Republican, he was both preceded and succeeded by Grover Cleveland, the only Democrat elected between 1860 and 1912. The administration of President Benjamin Harrison was characterized by the passage of the McKinley high protective tariff. The growth of large industrial combines was seemingly untouched by the passage of the ineffectual Sherman Anti-Trust Act. The stage was set for the labor unrest that followed the Panic of 1893 in the second Cleveland Administration.

The Harrison family produced two presidents. **William Henry Harrison**, the very short-lived (32 days) ninth president was the first president of his line, elected in 1844 as the first successful Whig Party candidate. Belying his claim to be born in a log cabin, he was a scion of one of the leading families of Virginia. The Harrison plantation on the James River below Richmond claims to be the site of the first Thanksgiving in America in 1619. It thereby precedes the one generally acknowledged to be first at Plymouth in Massachusetts.

Mostly associated with the Northwest Territory, Harrison was acclaimed as the hero of the Battle of Tippecanoe in 1811 at the Shawnee Indian village under Tecumseh and his brother The Prophet. During the War of 1812, at the Battle of the Thames in Ontario in 1813, the important Shawnee chief Tecumseh was killed. Elected president as a Whig in 1840, he was succeeded following his death just a few weeks in office by his manqué Democratic vice-president John Tyler.

Rutherford B. Hayes, the 19th president, was born in Ohio in 1822 in a family that had migrated from Vermont. He was raised by his widowed mother in close association with his maternal uncle. He trained at Kenyon College and Harvard Law School. He moved to Cincinnati in 1850 where he made his reputation in the defense of slaves seeking freedom in violation of the Fugitive Slave Act. As an abolitionist, he joined the Republican Party and the 23rd Ohio Volunteers at the start of the Civil War. He fought in the Army of the Potomac, was wounded at South Mountain in September 1862 and fought then in the Shenandoah Campaigns of 1864 under General **Philip Sheridan.**

Elected to Congress in 1864, he was a member of the 39th Congress that passed the 14th Amendment and instituted military Reconstruction in opposition to President Andrew Johnson. Elected Ohio Governor in 1867, he supported ratification by Ohio of the 15th Amendment establishing Negro suffrage.

The Republican presidential candidate in the 1876 election, the contested electoral votes that assured his election were part of a bargain to withdraw the still remaining Federal troops supporting Reconstruction in the former Confederate states. His term ending in 1881 was colored by the apparently fraudulent process by which he achieved office. Nevertheless, he began the process of reforming the civil service accomplished only in 1883 in the subsequent administration of President Chester Arthur.

Garret Hobart was born in 1844 in Long Branch New Jersey and grew up in Marlboro New Jersey. He studied at Rutgers College, graduating in 1863. He did not serve in the Union Army. He read law with an influential family friend in Paterson New Jersey, married the daughter and became wealthy in corporate practice. Highly congenial, he entered Republican New Jersey state politics, rising to Speaker in the General Assembly and then President of the New Jersey Senate. At the 1896 Republican Convention, his delegation supported him for the vice-presidential nomination. Mark Hanna accepted him as the nominee since his views were similar to that of the presidential nominee **William McKinley.** Hobart died in office with Theodore Roosevelt his successor as vice-president in McKinley's second term.

Sam Houston was born in 1793 in the Shenandoah Valley of Virginia and migrated with his family to east Tennessee. He ran away from home and lived among the nearby Cherokees and with whom he lived once again when they were forced to move to Arkansas. He fought in the War of 1812 when he came to the attention of Andrew Jackson who then sponsored him in his political career in Tennessee as member of the U.S. Congress. Because of personal difficulties, he left Tennessee to move to Texas, then part of Mexico.

Joining the Texan independence movement, he was the victor in the Battle of San Jacinto in 1836 that secured Texan independence. President of Texas, he advocated annexation by the United States. After annexation in 1845, Houston was a U.S. Senator, supported the Compromise of 1850, opposed the Kansas-Nebraska Act of 1854 and, as Governor unsuccessfully opposed the secession of Texas in 1861.

Andrew Jackson was the seventh president from 1833 to 1839. Born in 1767 to Scotch-Irish immigrants on the western frontier of the Carolinas, he lived mainly in Tennessee. Active in state politics, he was also a land speculator and member of the elite planter class with his plantation near Nashville. Commander of the militia forces, he conquered the Creek Indians and then the Seminoles in Florida. He was particularly famous as the hero of the Battle of New Orleans in 1815 during the War of 1812.

He was deprived by the vote of the House of Representatives of his election to the presidency in 1824 despite his plurality of the popular vote. He was then elected in 1828 by what was the former Jeffersonian Democratic-Republican Party, now rechristened as the Democratic Party. The 20th century Democratic Party under President Franklin Roosevelt claimed an affinity to its Jacksonian as well as its Jeffersonian roots. The original "self-made" man, Andrew Jackson was the first of the new breed who represented the principle of popular sovereignty and the common man in his concept of the role of the president and in his effort to destroy the Second Bank of the United States. In response to his actions, the Whig Party arose to represent the descendants of the earlier Federalist Party. Unlike the Jacksonian Democratic Party, the Whigs followed a program of internal improvements and successfully contested several presidential elections during the 1840s

John Jay was born in 1745 in New York City to a wealthy merchant family. He graduated from King's College in 1764 where his closest friend was Robert Livingston. Although initially a conservative, he became increasingly associated with American independence, took part in the Continental Congress and was appointed Minister to Spain in 1779. He helped negotiate the Treaty of Paris in 1783 recognizing American independence and was appointed Secretary of Foreign Affairs of the Confederation from 1784 to 1789.

Along with Alexander Hamilton and James Madison, he participated in writing the *Federalist Papers* advocating ratification of the U.S. Constitution. Appointed the first Chief Justice of the Supreme Court in 1789, he also negotiated in 1794 the Jay Treaty with Great Britain that was denounced by the anti-Federalist Jeffersonians as too favorable to British interests.

Thomas Jefferson was the third president from 1801-1809. Born in 1743 on the family plantation in the Piedmont region of Virginia, he trained at the College of William & Mary. A delegate from Virginia to the Continental Congress, Jefferson is credited with the leadership in writing the Declaration of Independence. He was also governor of Virginia during the

Revolutionary War, Minister to Paris from 1784 to 1789, Washington's first Secretary of State from 1790 to 1793 and founder of the Democratic-Republican Party. Elected vice-president in 1796 with John Adams as president, Jefferson opposed the Alien and Sedition Acts and carried out the first transfer of power from the governing Federalists when he became president in the election of 1800.

The credo of his party based its concept of liberty upon the maintenance of the small holder farmer. Although emphasizing limited government as the credo of his party and administration, he nevertheless doubled the size of the United States by buying Louisiana from Napoleon in 1803. This assured the highly important control of the Mississippi basin and its outlet at New Orleans for the benefit of the farmers of that area. It also seemed to assure the availability of land deemed necessary to support the extension of that yeoman class. Jefferson also sponsored the Lewis & Clark Expedition to survey this entire area. Reaching the Columbia River and the Pacific coast at Oregon, Lewis and Clark also helped insure American claims to that territory. At his death, Jefferson wished to be remembered on his gravestone as the Author of the Declaration of Independence, the Founder of the University of Virginia and the Author of the Virginia Statute for Religious Freedom.

Daniel of St Thomas Jenifer was born in 1723 on the family plantation near Port Tobacco in Charles County Maryland. A large landowner, he was on the Governor's Council. Nevertheless, he joined the cause of independence and represented Maryland in the Continental Congress. An elder statesman like his friend Benjamin Franklin at the Constitutional Convention in 1787, he supported a strong central government able to levy taxes.

Andrew Johnson was born in 1808 in North Carolina of poor parents. Unschooled, he was apprenticed to a tailor. He eventually settled in 1827 in Greenville in eastern Tennessee where he married the woman who taught him to write. Because of his origins, he was not accepted by the local gentry despite his rise in political office. An unabashed populist, in 1835 he was elected by his fellow poor whites as their champion in the Tennessee Legislature; in 1842 to the U.S. Congress as the first artisan ever elected from a slave state. Elected governor of Tennessee in 1853, as a man of the people he refused a carriage and walked to his inauguration. In 1857, he was elected U.S. Senator.

A small slave holder, he was a Southern Democratic Unionist like many of his eastern Tennessee constituents, different from those in the other parts of the state that had assured a two-thirds majority for secession. Johnson's hatred of the ruling planter class was matched only by his deep love of the Union. Unique among the representatives of those states that joined the Confederacy, he chose to remain in the U.S. Senate and to speak, "in the spirit of Andrew Jackson", forcefully against secession.

The prototype Southern Unionist, he was also for a time a member of the Joint Committee for the Conduct of the War that criticized General McClellan for his desultory ways. McClellan had the aim that the defeat of the Confederacy by the Army of the Potomac in the spring of 1862 would re-establish the Union, as much as possible as it was. That too remained Johnson's aim throughout his later presidency.

In February 1862, Johnson resigned his seat to be appointed military governor of Tennessee in newly captured Nashville. Surrounded by Confederates waging guerilla war and occasionally besieged in the city, Johnson stood for the Union against the secessionist large slave holders he called "traitorous." Although Tennessee was exempted on his request from the Emancipation Proclamation in 1862, by the end of 1863 he was supportive both of emancipation and the enlistment of black troops.

With the reputation so gained as the leading "War Democrat," Johnson was welcomed by Lincoln as the vice-presidential candidate on the "National Union" ticket in the 1864 election. At the inaugural in March 1865, Johnson acted incoherently in a way aberrant to his normal much more studied way. He spoke ungrammatically in the native accent of his plebian origins while also appearing drunk. Soon he was the president after the assassination of the sainted Lincoln,

The process for reinstatement of the seceded states had been conflicted from as early as 1861 regarding the role of the Executive versus Legislative Branch. The "easy" return of the seceded states into the Union derived from the concept that the Confederacy had never existed. This stance was held throughout the war by Lincoln; the population was merely in rebellion because of treasonous political leadership. Therefore, he held that as commander-in-chief, he could merely punish the traitors and then empower loyal Union men to resume the previous relationship of a state to the Union. The use of the term "Civil War" to describe that situation inferred such a set of principles.

Yet the individual Confederate soldiers were not treated as traitors; and the Confederacy was indeed treated as a legal entity. Was it not, as argued by the radical Republicans, a conquered territory to be rebuilt? The conflict was between easy "resumption" and a "reconstruction" that was more thoroughgoing,

Lincoln had been unsuccessful in recognizing merely by presidential decree the western counties as the breakaway government of Virginia;

rather the new state of West Virginia was created by Congress in late 1862. Lincoln did appoint military governors to manage civil affairs in the conquered territory but could not compel Congress to accept representatives from those areas. Nevertheless, his policy seemed to succeed in Louisiana; the Congress seated representatives elected in 1863. In December 1863, Lincoln thus issued his amnesty plan to follow the oath of allegiance of at least 10% of the number voting in 1860. In response, Congress refused to continue to seat the Louisiana representatives; in the summer of 1864, it issued its own more stringent Wade-Davis Plan. Lincoln's pocket veto and his own uncertain political future prior to the November 1864 election put a halt to further progress in resolving the entire issue.

Johnson followed the road apparently taken by Lincoln but without the latter's flexibility in achieving the possibly irreconcilable twin goals of reconciliation and protection of the rights of the newly freed. Having remained in the Senate after the secession of his state, Johnson himself took the stance that Tennessee, for example, had never left the Union. No state could legally secede. They could not go out, but they had. Johnson in the chaotic spring of 1865, acting without consultation with Congress, issued a Proclamation of broad amnesty for former Confederates. Starting with North Carolina, another proclamation provided for the reinstatement of state governments merely by repudiating the Confederate state debts, rescission of the ordinance of secession and ratification of the 13th Amendment abolishing slavery.

Voting rights for even a select group of educated Negroes was suggested but not required. The suffrage issue was complicated by the restriction on black suffrage that existed in many Northern states. Moreover, any land redistribution was quickly stopped. Johnson was proceeding unilaterally without consultation with Congress but was also negating the results of the war by reinstating the former ruling group that had led the Confederacy. Johnson had never been anything but a Southern Democrat representing the values of his class of white southerners. He had apparently come to support emancipation as a war measure. However, concern about Negro legal, political and economic rights was foreign to him.

Like many self-made men, he was stubborn in his stances; he disdained advice. It was President Johnson's considered opinion that the war had been fought to save the Union; that issue had now been resolved. The rights reserved to the states concerning voting and other aspects by the Constitution were still to be upheld as the basic law of the Union. The southern states can re-enter that union with all their rights assured now that their citizens were again loyal tax payers. In his sense of rectitude, Johnson steeled himself to act consistent with his limited view ignoring the wider implications of the emancipation created by the war.

However, it was clear to others that the Union victory in the Civil War had not merely settled the issue of secession; it had also included the moral issue of the destruction of slavery. For those others, many in Congress labeled by their opponents as "radical" Republicans, effective Emancipation had to be buttressed by civil rights, suffrage and possibly even by economic redress via distribution of abandoned land. Moreover, a viable Republican Party in the South based on Negro suffrage was a political necessity to safeguard the continuation of Republican Party power forged by the war.

Johnson was preoccupied during the summer of 1865 in personally issuing pardons to those officers, officials and the wealthy not covered by his blanket amnesty. The formerly rich and powerful came to him on bended knee, to be judged and treated occasionally in an overbearing way, with royal caprice. Now forgotten were his previous cries for harsh vengeance when he had military governor of Tennessee. It may be that in his mind he had indeed exacted his vengeance. He was not only the equal of those who had looked down upon him but their savior. They acclaimed him as such throughout the South and in his own town from which his family had previously been exiled. He had finally achieved the acceptance he had craved.

In February 1866, Johnson vetoed the Freedmen's Bureau Extension Bill, which contained a provision to have its powers strengthened on behalf of protecting the rights of the newly freed. He claimed that it was leading to excessive preferential treatment of Negroes. That veto was sustained. However, the veto of Civil Rights Bill, a direct response to the "black codes" that had been reinstituted in the South to control the freedmen, was overruled. The conflict with the Congress over the implications of the Civil War and Reconstruction had started. The mid-term election of 1866 led to the veto-proof Republican 40th Congress that eventually issued a Bill of Impeachment.

Andrew Johnson's impact on the outcome of the Civil War was far more momentous than the details of the ultimately unsuccessful impeachment trial that has generally been the focus. His actions were ultimately highly effective. They gave hope to the conquered South at a crucial time that their cause would not ultimately be lost. They would indeed regain power to undo the wider social changes engendered by their defeat.

Amos Kendall was born in 1789 and trained at Dartmouth College. He was the editor of the *Argus of Western America*, a progressive voice in Kentucky. A friend of Andrew Jackson, he was Postmaster General in charge of patronage for both Presidents Jackson and Van Buren. He helped Francis Preston Blair found the *Washington Globe* as the voice of the Jacksonians. After supporting the subsidy for the work of Samuel Morse, Kendall became president of the Western Union Telegraph Company. Among his philanthropies was the founding of the Columbian Institution for the Deaf and the recruitment of Edward Miner Gallaudet to head it.

Martin Luther King Jr. was born in Atlanta Georgia in 1929. He entered Atlanta's Morehouse College at age fifteen and later attended Crozer Theological Seminary in Pennsylvania before receiving a Ph.D. from the Boston University School of Theology. Said to be deeply influenced by the Dean of the Boston University Chapel Harold Thurman toward Gandhian non-violence, he became pastor of the Dexter Avenue Baptist Church in Montgomery Alabama in 1954. He led the Montgomery Bus Boycott there. Moving back to Atlanta in 1960, under the auspices of the Southern Christian Leadership Conference (SCLC) that he founded, he became recognized as a leader in many of the civil rights protests during the early 1960s. The 1963 March on Washington culminating in his *I Have a Dream* speech at the Lincoln Memorial, expressed the hope for racial conciliation that was made explicit in the civil rights legislation of the 1960s. His assassination in 1968 followed his less successful attempt to extend his ministry to issues of poverty and peace as well as continued racial discrimination in the North.

Daniel S. Lamont was born in Cortland County New York in 1851. He attended Union College in Schenectady. Closely associated with Grover Cleveland when New York Governor, Lamont followed him to Washington. He was Secretary of War from 1893 to 1897 in President Cleveland's second term. He then became president of the Northern Pacific Railroad.

Abraham Lincoln was born in Kentucky in a log cabin in 1809, moved to Indiana and then Illinois. Unschooled, he nevertheless became a successful lawyer in Springfield Illinois. Elected to Congress for one term as a Whig in 1844, he became a champion of the Free-Soil doctrine opposed to the spread of slavery. He came to national attention in his unsuccessful run as Republican candidate for the U.S. Senate in 1858 via the Lincoln-Douglas Debates. He was the compromise "moderate" Republican candidate for president in 1860. His election was guaranteed by the split in the Democratic Party. Despite his moderate stance vis a vis slavery in that he opposed merely its spread, his election was taken as a signal for secession by the South. His leadership during the Civil War both as a commander-in-chief and political leader was instrumental in winning the Civil War. His humanity during the war and commitment to abolition of slavery culminating in the 13th Amendment has made him since his assassination in April 1865 the best-loved American president.

Robert R. Livingston was born on the family estate of Livingston Manor on the Hudson River in 1748. He graduated from King's College (predecessor of Columbia College) in 1765. Appointed Chancellor of New York (the highest judicial office) from 1777, he chose to carry that title for the rest of his life. A member of the Continental Congress, he was part of the committee that drafted the Declaration of Independence, but did not sign that document because of the opposition of his colony. He was the first Secretary of Foreign Affairs for the Confederation from 1781-1783. In his role as Chancellor, he administered the oath of office to George Washington at his first inaugural.

An adherent to the Jeffersonian Democratic-Republican party, he was appointed Minister to France from 1801-1804 and credited with the negotiations that led to the Louisiana Purchase. While in Paris, he became acquainted with Robert Fulton. Together, they started the first commercial steamship service from New York to Albany with a stop at his ancestral estate at Clermont Landing (also the name of the ship).

James Madison was the fourth president from 1809 to 1817. Born in Orange County Virginia in 1751 on the family plantation of Montpellier, he was closely associated with Thomas Jefferson throughout his career. He trained at the College of New Jersey (later Princeton) under George Witherspoon, Edinburgh trained. One of the youngest delegates, Madison was importantly involved in the Constitutional Convention and then, along with Alexander Hamilton and John Jay, in its ratification with the writing of *The Federalist Papers*. A member of the House of Representatives in the early Congresses, he helped assure passage of the Bill of Rights, particularly in the passage of the 1st amendment similar to the Virginia Statute of Religious Freedom.

He was the leader in the founding of the anti-Federalist Democratic-Republican Party in the U.S. Congress. Secretary of State from 1801 to 1809 under President Thomas Jefferson, he led in the efforts to maintain American commerce vis a vis the actions of the warring powers during the Napoleonic Wars. With the failure of the policy of "peaceable coercion" with its embargo and non-importation acts, his own presidency was marred by the War of 1812. The poorly trained and equipped U.S. Army failed in its expedition to conquer Canada and was unable to protect the national capital from capture by the British in 1814. Dolley Madison, his wife and famous First Lady, is credited with saving the famous portrait of George Washington when the White House was burned.

William McKinley was born in Niles Ohio in 1843. His family members were former ironworkers from western Pennsylvania. Their Whig and abolitionist sentiments as well as Methodist religion remained defining characteristics throughout his career. He enlisted in what became the 23rd Ohio Volunteer Regiment as a private in the spring of 1861 and fought, along with his mentor Rutherford B. Hayes, throughout the war. His wartime service was mainly in West Virginia and the Shenandoah Valley campaigns and most notably at the Battles of South Mountain and Antietam in September 1862.

After studying law at the Albany Law School, he settled in Canton Ohio. There he entered local Republican politics and acted in support of his friend Rutherford Hayes during the contested election of 1876. Entering Congress that same year, he remained there, with some interruptions, rising to the leadership of the important Ways and Means Committee. He came under the patronage of the Republican leader Mark Hanna, the wealthy Cleveland industrialist who backed him for the presidency in 1896.

The 25th president, he was the last of the roll call of Republicans elected post Civil War on the platform of the protective tariff, the gold standard and generous Civil War Union veterans' pensions. Marked by the victorious Spanish-American War in 1898, his time in office was the start of the American Pacific Ocean Empire including the annexation of Hawaii and the Philippines. Assassinated in 1901 early during his second term, he was succeeded by Theodore Roosevelt.

John Marshall was born in 1755 in what was then the frontier in Fauquier County Virginia. His father, an agent of Lord Fairfax, provided him with access to the latter's extensive library. After service in the Continental Army during the Revolutionary War, he read law with George Wythe at the College of William & Mary. Settled in Richmond, he advocated ratification of the U.S. Constitution in opposition to the anti-Federalists like Patrick Henry. For a short time Secretary of State under President John Adams, he brought to an end the "Quasi-War" with France. He was appointed Chief Justice in 1801 just before the Jeffersonian Party took over the presidency. In office until 1835, he created the role of the Court to rule on the constitutionality of laws.

James Monroe, the fifth president from 1817 to 1825, was born in 1758 on a plantation in Westmoreland County acquired by his Scottish immigrant ancestor in the 17th century. He was famously Minister to Paris at the time of the Louisiana Purchase in 1803, Secretary of State and Secretary of War in the Madison Administration during the War of 1812 and the burning of Washington. The last president of the Virginia dynasty; with the demise of the Federalist Party, he was unopposed for the presidency. His tenure is famous for the Monroe Doctrine in 1823 that declared the Western Hemisphere off limits to European conquest under the protection of the United States. The major domestic action was the Missouri Compromise of 1820 that defined the limits of expansion of slavery in the territory acquired in the Louisiana Purchase

Levi Morton, vice-president along with President Benjamin Harrison from 1889 to 1893, was born in Shoreham Vermont in 1824. A successful businessman in Boston and then New York, he was a Republican member of Congress in the late 1870s and then appointed Minister to France by President James Garfield from 1881to 1884. While vice-president, he rebuilt his home that still remains on its site on Scott Circle. He also built an early version of the Hotel Shoreham, naming it after the town of his birth.

James Otis Jr. was born in West Barnstable Massachusetts in 1725 to a leading jurist. Graduated from Harvard in 1743, he was a leading lawyer when in 1761 he opposed the "writs of assistance" by which the British claimed the right to enter homes without reason or recourse. His long speech galvanized the revolutionary spirit by basing colonial rights on the *Magna Carta* and the British Constitution. A leader in the Revolutionary movement, he was a member of the Stamp Act Congress in 1765 but opposed the more radical Samuel Adams.

John S. Phelps was born in Hartford County Connecticut in 1814 and graduated from Trinity College in 1832. He moved to Springfield Missouri in 1837. Elected to the U.S. Congress from 1845 to 1863, he was chair of the Ways and Means Committee. He joined the U.S. Army in 1861 and led his regiment to victory at Pea Ridge in Arkansas in March 1862. One of Missouri's greatest governors, he was elected in 1876 to heal the breach between the northern and southern factions.

Franklin Pierce was born in Hillsborough New Hampshire in 1804 to a politically prominent family. He trained at Phillips' Exeter Academy and Bowdoin College in 1824 where his classmates included Nathaniel Hawthorne and Henry Wadsworth Longfellow. Active in Democratic politics in New Hampshire, he was elected to Congress from 1833 to 1837 and to the U.S. Senate from 1837 to 1842. He served in the Mexican War under General Winfield Scott in the conquest of Mexico City. In 1852, a Northerner with Southern sympathies, he was selected by a dead-locked convention as a compromise Democratic candidate for president. His one-term presidency was disrupted by the Kansas-Nebraska Act of 1854 that repealed the Missouri Compromise by opening those territories to slavery in the name of "popular sovereignty."

James K. Polk was born in Mecklenburg County North Carolina in 1795 and is primarily identified with Tennessee. A protégé of Andrew Jackson, he was governor of Tennessee before being elected president in 1844. During his one term, he succeeded in the annexation of the Republic of Texas, settling the Oregon dispute with Britain and waging the Mexican War. The term "Manifest Destiny" was coined during his presidency to justify the drive to incorporate into the United States the land "from sea to shining sea."

Josiah Quincy was born in Boston in 1772 the namesake of a Revolutionary War patriot. He trained at Phillips' Andover Academy and graduated from Harvard in 1790. A lawyer, he was active in Massachusetts state politics and Federalist member of Congress from 1805 to 1813. Known as the "Last Federalist," he was mayor of Boston from 1823 to 1829 and president of Harvard College from 1829 to 1845.

Edmund Randolph was born in 1753 in Williamsburg Virginia. A member of the influential Randolph family, he graduated from the College of William & Mary in 1775 and read law with his father John and uncle Peyton. Unlike his Loyalist father, Edmund Randolph remained in America and joined the Continental Army and was for a time aide to General George Washington. A delegate from Virginia to the Continental Congress from 1779 to 1782, he was also one of that state's delegation to the Constitutional Convention in 1787. There his "Virginia Plan" was the basis for the development of the Constitution including Article III establishing the federal court system, absent in the Articles of Confederation.

He was appointed Attorney General by President George Washington and succeeded his cousin Thomas Jefferson as the second Secretary of State in 1793. The Jay Treaty, negotiated during his tenure, was signed by him but was actually the work of Alexander Hamilton.

Peyton Randolph was born in Williamsburg in 1721, trained at the College of William & Mary and studied law at the Middle Temple of the Inns of the Court in London in 1743. Returning to Virginia, he was appointed Attorney General and also elected to Virginia House of Burgesses. Despite possible conflict of interest, he opposed the implementation of the Townshend Acts; as Speaker of the House of Burgesses, he convened a meeting of the burgesses after their dissolution by the royal governor.

Theodore Roosevelt (TR) was born in 1858 to a wealthy family of Dutch extraction long settled in New York. However, his mother was an unreconstructed Southern belle from Roswell Georgia. He graduated from Harvard College in 1876. His first book, *The Naval War* of 1812 was written with the aid of James Bullock, his maternal uncle. The latter had been an important Confederate agent in Great Britain responsible for the outfitting of warships to break the Union blockade.

The simultaneous death of his first wife and mother drove TR to leave New York to become a rancher in the West. On his return, he first became noted in 1895 when he became a reform New York Police Commissioner. When appointed Assistant Secretary of the Navy in 1897 by President William McKinley, he needed no introduction to the issue of naval power. It had been formed by his boyhood association with his maternal uncles and his book on the war of 1812. While the Secretary of the Navy was relatively inactive, Roosevelt prepared the navy for war. He was a member of an informal group centered about the person and the doctrines of naval Captain Alfred Thayer Mahan. Mahan was the author of *The Influence of Sea Power on History, 1660-1783*, a seminal book in 1890 on the primacy of the navy to protect American interests. Roosevelt saw the importance of a two-ocean navy with a canal through Central America necessary to permit easy deployment. He also saw the strategic importance of American ownership of Hawaii to prevent Japanese control of the Pacific.

The destruction of the battleship *Maine* in Havana Harbor in February 1898 had gone unanswered by Spain; newspapers had been screaming for vengeance. Finally, in April 1898, war was declared. Prior to joining the army, to see action in Cuba, Roosevelt, long prepared for the war, instructed Admiral Dewey to proceed from Hong Kong to Manila. The great victory in Manila Bay assured American control of the Philippines and the Pacific.

Roosevelt had long longed to erase the stain of his father's having bought a substitute for serving in the Union army during the Civil War. Second-in-command under Colonel Leonard Wood of the 1st Volunteer Cavalry Regiment; with Wood raised to brigade commander, the unit became Roosevelt's. His "Rough Riders," styled after part of the title of Buffalo Bill's Wild West Show, were the first men ashore in an attack on Santiago on the east end of the island. Journalists conveniently accompanying the unit, cabled that Colonel Roosevelt had been brave, his leadership brilliant. He next led in the taking of "San Juan Hill' to be immortalized by the famous war correspondent Richard Harding Davis that led to TR's recommendation for the Medal of Honor. A timid child by nature and early upbringing, he had, by sheer will, made himself fearless.

In running for New York Governor in 1898, Roosevelt barnstormed throughout the state in a fashion that would characterize all his subsequent campaigns. Once elected, his efforts foretold his later priorities: to aid in conservation, to help the laboring man and clean up politics by uncoupling party machinery from business tribute. His major accomplishment was establishing a tax on public franchises such as utilities despite the opposition of New York City financiers. In order to get him out of Albany, the Republican Party machine insured his nomination to the useless role of vice-president in the election of 1900.

While McKinley carried out a "front-porch" campaign in Canton Ohio, Roosevelt traveled throughout the country greeting millions of voters. While wrapping the Republican Party in the American flag, he denied that the ongoing war against the insurrection in the Philippines was by its very nature imperialistic. The Republican victory was overwhelming and Roosevelt had been placed in the cul de sac of the vice-presidency

The Republican Party's regulars had their worst fears realized when Roosevelt ascended to the presidency after McKinley's assassination in September 1900. Everything in his philosophy of strength had assured him that he would enter the White House someday; He had fought all his life for that which is most arduous, not shrinking from danger or hardship. Always in a hurry, he was now president at age forty-four, the youngest in history. His own biological weakness, conquered only with great difficulty, reinforced his belief in the cult of the "survival of the fittest," so popular in his time. His adherence to the strenuous in personal life extended to the need for military preparedness in relation to the United States and, coupled with his belief in white supremacy and moral obligation, led to his version of American imperialism.

Roosevelt claimed the Republican Lincoln as his presidential model as an active Executive. As a mark of his devotion, Roosevelt wore a ring that contained hair taken from Lincoln's head when he died. TR made a career of politics at a time when well-bred Harvard men shunned its depravity. Roosevelt dealt with votes, elections and party regularity because he loved power. Power would bring order; with order, there is the opportunity for the moral life. The men who were in power must be moral; their morality arose from character either via generations of good breeding or by long seasons of hard work. He saw himself as meeting both criteria. He created a new version of conservatism but used the Republican Party to be his vehicle rather than the Democratic Party so associated with the corrupt city machines such as Tammany Hall in New York City.

His foreign policy was the wielding of power but now derived from military preparedness to maintain order; there was the clash of nations in a world from which America could not be isolated. "Manifest Destiny" now applied beyond the traditional borders of the United States. His first action would be to insure American control of an isthmian canal as part of his grand naval strategy. Favoring the shorter route in Panama over Nicaragua, he insured the success of Panama's most recent insurrection from Colombia in return for the canal route. The Panama Canal was an American engineering triumph where the French had failed. It has been compared to the making of the atomic bomb in World War II and the moon walk in the 1960s.

The subsequent round the world voyage of the American battle fleet was designed to warn Japan of American power in the Pacific while his intervention in settling the Russo-Japanese War served to maintain the balance of power in the Orient. He accepted evolution through struggle as basic to all life; its course could not be altered. He assigned a high role for the Anglo-Saxon race as born to rule since the British did rule so much of the world and had, in America, conquered the continent.

Trees had always been of special value to him, particularly when filled with birdsong. He had planted trees on the bare hillsides of his family home on Long Island. His commitment to conservation served the orderly development of land and water resources by his public power and irrigation policies. Roosevelt's work as a conservationist was more lasting than any other. It fit his own personal interests, his deep friendship with Gifford Pinchot, the head of the Forest Service and a moral stance above party interests. To the undying enmity of the West, before signing a bill prepared to insure that no further reserves would be created in the western states, Roosevelt placed millions of acres under Federal control before signing the bill in question. He created five National Parks including Crater Lake in California; sixteen National Monuments including Muir Woods and numerous Wildlife Refuges.

Probably Roosevelt's most difficult battle was with himself in his decision not to seek re-election in 1908. He was a man who loved power and loved using it. He now chose not to run. Although actually elected only once, he had served almost an two entire terms. He compared himself and was compared only to George Washington in his selflessness in the name of the traditional two term limits to the presidency. He came to rue his choice of William Howard Taft, his Secretary of War, to pursue Roosevelt's still highly controversial and largely beset policies.

Analostan Island in the Potomac opposite Georgetown was acquired as Theodore Roosevelt Island to serve as a nature preserve in recognition of his role in building the National Parks system and also to contain his memorial. Earlier a model plantation owned by John Mason with a Federal-style house, it had gone back to nature. Completed in 1967, a greater than life portrait statue shows Theodore Roosevelt on his hustings delivering a speech with his arm outstretched. The sculptor Paul Manship was trained in Rome. Highly influenced by Egyptian antiquities, Manship's work was compatible with the art deco of the 1930s. He is most noted for the Prometheus Fountain in Rockefeller Center.

William W. Seaton was born in 1785 in King William County Virginia. Along with his brother-in-law Joseph Gales, he was the proprietor of the *National Intelligencer*, the recorder of the debates of the U.S. Congress from 1798 to 1837 and generally considered to be the voice of the Administration during the era of the war of 1812. Later a Whig, Seaton was the mayor of Washington from 1840 to 1850.

William Seward was born in New York in 1801 to a prosperous family. He studied law at Union College and then entered into partnership with his lawyer father-in-law in Auburn New York. Along with his friend Thurlow Weed, he entered the New York State Senate in the 1830s and was then elected Governor in 1838 for two terms. He was noted particularly for his work for prison reform. An abolitionist since early childhood, he and his wife used their home as a safe house on the Underground Railroad. Elected to the U.S Senate as a Whig in 1849, he became recognized as a leader against the "Slave Power," defended runaway slaves under the Fugitive Slave Act and spoke of the "irrepressible conflict" between the slave and free parts of the country.

Now a Republican, he expected in 1860 to win the nomination for president rather than the more "moderate" Abraham Lincoln. Appointed Secretary of State, he was the leading member of the Lincoln cabinet. He carried out the highly important role of keeping Britain and France from recognizing the Confederacy and intervening in the war. Loyal to Lincoln, he was the object of a nearly successful assassination attempt coincidental with the attack on Lincoln in April 1865. Continuing as a member of Andrew Johnson's cabinet, he was responsible in 1867 for the then much maligned purchase of Alaska from the Russians.

Alexander Shepherd was born in the less fashionable Southwest quadrant of the District of Columbia in 1835. Trained as a plumber, he owned his own firm. An early adherent to the Republican Party, he was a member of the Washington City Council from 1861. With the change to a Territorial form of government in 1871 that he favored, Shepherd became vice-chair of the semi-independent Board of Public Works; and in 1873 the second and last Governor of the District of Columbia. Under his auspices, a very active public works program carried out the grading and paving of streets, the planting of trees and the laying of water and sewer lines, all of which transformed the city into one that became attractive to the wealthy post-Civil War. The high cost of such improvements led to the eventual demise by Congress of local self-government in 1878 with the establishment of the appointive Commissioners that lasted until the 1960s.

John Sherman was born in Lancaster Ohio in 1823. He studied law and moved to Mansfield Ohio in 1844. He was active in Whig politics in the

1840s. Elected to the Congress in 1854 as a Republican, he remained until elected Senator in 1861 upon the resignation of Salmon Chase to become Secretary of the Treasury. He was the brother of General William T. Sherman. Head of the Senate Finance Committee, Sherman was appointed Secretary of the Treasury in 1877 by President **Rutherford Hayes**. Back in the Senate in 1888, Sherman remained Republican leader, instrumental in the passage in 1890 of the Sherman Anti-Trust Act. Because of his standing in the Republican Party, President **William McKinley** appointed him for a short time to be Secretary of State in 1897. He was also active in real estate development in the District of Columbia where the street named after him runs.

Roger Sherman was born in Newton in 1721 and grew up in Stoughton Massachusetts before moving to New Haven Connecticut in 1743. Unschooled, he later became a lawyer, member of the Connecticut House and Governor's Council in the 1760s. A member of the Continental Congress, he was one of the committee responsible for the writing of the Declaration of Independence. At the Constitutional Convention in 1787, he especially supported the primacy of the Legislature vis a vis the Executive. Moreover, he proposed the compromise that allowed for the small states having equal representation in the Senate and the large states greater representation in the House.

Edwin Stanton was born in 1814 in Steubenville Ohio. He went to Kenyon College and then read law. After practicing in Ohio and Pittsburgh, he moved to Washington in 1856. An Anti-Slavery Democrat, he was appointed Attorney-General in the last months of the Buchanan Administration and is credited during his time in office with opposing the uncontrolled drift to secession.

Appointed Secretary of War in January 1862 to replace **Simon Cameron**, his brusque uncompromising incorruptible manner helped achieve effective organization of the Union forces. The War Department building adjoined the White House to the west. The Telegraph Office resided there after March 1862 in the library immediately next to his office. By making the War Department's Telegraph Office his military nerve center, Lincoln became a Commander-in-chief like no other president before him and, along with Stanton, maintained civilian control of the military.

Remaining in office until 1867, Stanton clashed with President **Andrew Johnson** over Reconstruction. Protected by the Tenure of Office Act, he refused to resign despite the appointment of General Grant to take his place. This became one of the issues upon which President Johnson was tried in his Bill of Impeachment.

Charles Sumner was born in Boston in 1811 of abolitionist parents, attended Boston Latin School where the abolitionist Wendell Phillips was one of his friends. He further trained at Harvard College and then Harvard Law School. First elected to the Senate as a Democrat in 1850, he spoke forcefully against the Fugitive Slave Law in the Compromise of 1850 and against the Kansas-Nebraska Act in 1854. His verbal attack on one of the Southern authors of the latter led to a physical attack on him by the man's nephew, a congressional representative from South Carolina. Considered a martyr by the North after the attack, Sumner was re-elected as a Republican in 1856 and successively until the election of 1874. Chair of the Senate F9reign Relations Committee during the Civil War, he was also the leader of the "radical" Republicans in the U.S. Senate during the battle with President Andrew Johnson over control of Reconstruction.

William Howard Taft was born in 1857 to a well-established Cincinnati family. His father Alphonso, a leading Republican, held several appointments in the cabinet of President Ulysses Grant. Trained at Yale, he graduated from the Cincinnati Law School in 1880. He first came to Washington when appointed Solicitor General in 1890 by President Benjamin Harrison. Governor-General of the Philippines from 1901 to 1903, he was appointed in 1904 Secretary of War by President Theodore Roosevelt and anointed to be his reluctant successor as president in 1908. His lessened commitment to TR's progressive policies led to the split in the Republican Party and TR's independent Progressive Party candidacy in 1912. Taft finally found his much more congenial position as Chief Justice from 1921 to 1930. The important bridge that crosses the Rock Creek Valley to Connecticut Avenue carrying his name was initiated during his presidency.

Zachary Taylor, the 12th president, was born in 1784 on a plantation in Orange County Virginia. After his family's move west, he grew up relatively unlettered in Louisville Kentucky. He entered the U.S. Army in 1808, serving through the various Seminole Indian wars and the War of 1812 while simultaneously intermittently speculating in land and slaves. He is best known for his command during the Mexican War when he invaded from the Texan border, captured Monterrey and defeated Santa Ana at the Battle of Buena Vista in February 1847. A popular military hero in the tradition of Andrew Jackson, known as a citizen soldier rather than one trained at West Point, he was called "Rough and Ready." He declared himself a Whig and was elected in 1848. He died in office due to illness in 1850 to be succeeded by **Millard Fillmore.**

Samuel Tilden, born in New York in 1814, trained at Yale before graduating from New York University in 1837. A lawyer, he made his fortune in the 1850s while reorganizing railroads. After the Civil War, he became active in Democratic Party politics. In conflict with Tammany Hall and the notorious Tweed Ring in New York City, he succeeded in impeaching the corrupt judges sustaining their power. Elected as a reform-minded Governor of New York in 1874, he was the Democratic presidential candidate in 1876.

In the November 1876 presidential balloting, Samuel Tilden received a majority of the popular vote and 184 of the 185 electoral votes need to win. The Republican Party candidate, the Ohioan **Rutherford Hayes**, received only 165 votes but the 20 electoral votes that remained disputed in Oregon, Florida, Louisiana, and South Carolina. The last three were the only states in which federal troops were nominally still in place to oversee Reconstruction. Southerners on the Electoral Commission established to deal with the contested electoral votes knew that Tilden and Hayes would remove such troops. However, they sided with the Republican Hayes. Their support was in return for additional assurances that there would be federal money for internal improvements in the South including subsidies for the building of a southern railroad to the Pacific.

Benjamin F. Tracy was born in Oswego New York in 1830. He commanded the 109th New York Regiment winning a Medal of Honor at the Battle of the Wilderness in May 1864. He then commanded the 127th Infantry U.S. Colored Troops (USCT). After the war, he served on the New York Court of Appeals. Secretary of the Navy under President Benjamin Harrison, he helped create the "New Navy," initiating the building of battleships in accordance with the philosophy of Captain Alfred Thayer Mahan, author of highly influential *The Influence of Sea Power on History*.

Joseph Underwood was born in 1791 in Goochland County Virginia and moved to Kentucky in 1803. He graduated from Transylvania University in 1811, studied law and practiced in Glasgow and then Bowling Green Kentucky. He was elected several times to the Kentucky Legislature, as a Whig to the U.S. Congress from 18 35 to 1843 and to the U.S. Senate from 1847 to 1853.

Abel Upshur was born in 1790 on his family's plantation in Northampton County Virginia. He attended both Princeton and Yale, but failed to graduate from either. He read law and settled in Richmond Virginia. A stalwart conservative, he advocated states' rights and supported South Carolina during the "nullification" controversy of the 1830s. President John Tyler appointed him Secretary of the Navy in 1841. During his tenure, he established the Naval Observatory and Hydrological Office. Appointed Secretary of State by the same president in 1844, he worked closely with Texas in order to enable it to be annexed as a slave state, not to be finally accomplished until 1846 during the term of the next President James Polk.

Martin Van Buren was born in 1782 in a Dutch-speaking community near Albany New York called Kinderhook. He was active in New York politics and in the establishment of the Jacksonian Democratic Party. The eighth president from 1839 to 1843, he was a protégé of **Andrew Jackson**, Secretary of State from 1829 and his Vice-President during the second term during 1833 to 1837. The first president of Dutch ancestry, he was also the first born when the United States was already independent.

His administration was marred by the Panic of 1837, attributed by some to the destruction of the Second Bank of the United States by Andrew Jackson and the issuance of currency by the unfettered state banks. In 1848, he unsuccessfully ran for the presidency as the candidate of both the "Barnburner" section of the Democratic Party and the "Free Soil Party" opposed to the extension of slavery. His candidacy siphoned enough votes to give the presidency to the Democrat James K. Polk who proceeded to annex Texas as a slave state and wage the Mexican War.

John Peter Van Ness was born in 1770 in New York to a well-established family of Dutch origin. He studied at the Columbia College and came to Washington in 1800 to serve for a short time as a Jeffersonian party representative in Congress. **Martin Van Buren** was one of his protégés in their home town of Kinderhook. Married to Martha Burnes, the heir at that time to the largest fortune in the City of Washington, the Van Ness couple was active in the social and business scene. He was also involved in local politics as one-time mayor and in leadership of the local militia.

John M. Varnum was born in Dracut Massachusetts in 1778 and graduated from Harvard College in 1798. He practiced law in Haverhill and Lowell Massachusetts and was elected to the U.S. Congress from 1825 to 1831.

Richard Wallach was born in Alexandria in 1816, grew up in Washington, attended the Columbian College (now George Washington University) and was admitted to the bar in 1837. Appointed to a number of posts in the Washington local government, he was elected mayor in 1861 and served until 1868 throughout the time of the city's explosive growth during the Civil War. He was not re-elected with the advent in 1867 of the voting franchise by the freed Blacks.

George Washington was born in 1732 near Fredericksburg Virginia. His name is on his city that he also insured would reflect his vision as the capital of a great country. Although the presence of his monument pervades the city, there is little of George Washington in our street names. One sliver of a street carries his name at the base of Capitol Hill runs from Independence Avenue to South Capitol Street. It recalls the route taken by the now defunct "Washington Canal" that connected the Anacostia and Potomac Rivers through the city of Washington as an adjunct to the C&O Canal.

Daniel Webster was born in 1782 in what is now Franklin New Hampshire, went to Phillips' Exeter Academy and Dartmouth College. He was trained in law in Boston and his later career was in Massachusetts but he was originally elected to Congress from his native state in 1812. As a Federalist representing New England maritime interests, he opposed the War of 1812 and President Madison's war policies. A successful constitutional lawyer, he established in conjunction with the Supreme Court led by the Federalist John Marshall, many of the constitutional principles that remain in force.

Elected to the U.S. Senate from Massachusetts in 1827, he united along with Henry Clay against President Andrew Jackson to be one of the leading political figures of the Whig Party. Like Clay, he was a perennial candidate for nomination for president; unlike Clay, he was never the nominee. Twice turning down the option of becoming vice-president to men who died in office, he was instead selected as Secretary of State in both the Whig Administrations of William Henry Harrison (and for a time under President John Tyler) and that of Millard Fillmore. His major accomplishment was the negotiation of the Webster-Ashburton Treaty of 1842 settling the northeast border dispute between the United States and Canada.

His greatest of many speeches was his *Second Reply to Haynes* when he affirmed "Liberty and Union, now and forever, one and inseparable" in answer to his opponent's stance for states' rights: "The Union, secondary to Liberty most dear." His support among his New England constituents never recovered from his Seventh of March speech when he supported passage of the Fugitive Slave Law as part of the debate surrounding the Compromise of 1850.

Woodrow Wilson was born in Staunton Virginia in 1856 and grew up mainly in Augusta Georgia. A son of the South, his father was the leader of the Southern Presbyterian Church. He graduated from Princeton in 1879, attended the University of Virginia Law School but then received his doctorate from John Hopkins in 1886 with a dissertation on Congressional Government. Appointed Professor of Political Science at Princeton in 1890, he continued to write on the subject of his dissertation, the greater integration of the Executive and the Legislature on the model of the British Parliament.

President of Princeton in 1908, he tried unsuccessfully to modify the socially restrictive "eating club" system. Running as a reform candidate, he was elected Governor of New Jersey in 1910. He was nominated as the Democratic Party presidential candidate in 1912 only after 46 ballots and elected because of the split in the Republican Party by the Progressive Party candidacy of Theodore Roosevelt. His credo of "New Freedom" included control of banking with the Federal Reserve Act and better control of monopolies with the Clayton Anti-Trust Act and the Federal Trade Commission.

The European war starting in 1914 became his preoccupation. American entry int0 the war in April 1917 on the side of the Allied Powers brought about a high degree of mobilization including federal control of the railroads, industrial and food controls as well as large scale public bond sales. The commitment to self-determination of subject peoples embodied in the "Fourteen Points" brought about in the peace treaties after the end of the- then called Great War the dismemberment of the Austro-Hungarian Empire. His unsuccessful fight for American ratification of the League of Nations ended with his illness due to recurrent cerebral vascular disease.

His namesake bridge crosses the Potomac River between Maryland and Virginia as part of the interstate highway system that he advocated.

4.2 Military Figures

There are somewhat over thirty military figures whose names are placed on the streets of Washington, There are many from the Revolutionary War era and the few from the mainly naval heroes of War of 1812. The largest number from the Civil War era is closely associated with the circles that also contain their highly visible statues.

Joshua Barney was born in Baltimore in 1759. He fought in the Continental Navy during the Revolutionary War and re-entered the U.S. Navy at the start of the War of 1812. Commander of the Chesapeake Bay Flotilla of small boats, he attacked the British fleet in 1814 as it approached Washington. The Marines previously stationed on his abandoned ships provided the major but inadequately small defense line at the Battle of Bladensburg. They could not prevent the capture of Washington and the burning of its public buildings in August 1814.

John Barry, one of the founders of the U.S. Navy. was Irish-born to a poor tenant farmer in 1745. A merchant captain, he was commander of the important Continental Navy ship *Alliance* during the Revolutionary War. In 1794, he was appointed senior captain in the U.S. Navy in command of the *USS United States*. During the Quasi-War with France in 1798-1801 with the rank of Commodore, he commanded the U.S. naval forces in the Caribbean.

Benjamin Butler was born in 1818 in Deerfield New Hampshire, graduated from Waterville College in Maine (now Colby College) in 1838, read law and practiced in Lowell Massachusetts. Without military training

73

but head of the Massachusetts militia, he commanded the 6th Massachusetts Regiment in April 1861 that was attacked while transiting Baltimore to aid the beleaguered national capital. He then occupied Baltimore and declared martial law.

An important Democrat, he received an appointment by President Lincoln as a "political" general in the Union Army. Commanding Fortress Monroe on the Chesapeake, as early as May 1861 he made the crucial decision to declare as "contraband" slaves fleeing to the Union lines. Once again, when in New Orleans, he permitted the enlistment of the free Blacks previously part of the Confederate forces to be part of the Union forces, the first such. Less successful in his actual military role, he became infamous as "Beast Butler" in riding roughshod over the women of occupied New Orleans.

George Rogers Clark was born in Charlottesville Virginia in 1752 and grew up in Caroline County on the family plantation. He surveyed land in what later became Kentucky and fought Indians as head of the Kentucky militia in the Revolutionary War. His greatest success was the capture of Kaskaskia and Vincennes in 1778 that led to him being considered "The Father of the Northwest Territory." After the war, like other veterans, he was granted large tracts of land in Indiana. Clarksville in Clark County remains in his memory.

Stephen Decatur was born in 1779 while his father, a merchant captain, was a U.S. Naval officer in the Revolutionary War. Decatur joined the U.S. Navy as a midshipman in 1798 serving under Commodore Barry while involved in the Quasi-War with France under President John Adams. He was a lieutenant in the First War with the Barbary Pirates while Thomas Jefferson was president, famous for his daring raid on the captured U.S.S. Philadelphia in the harbor of Tripoli. He was a captain of the *USS United States* in the War of 1812 noted for his defeat of the *H.M.S. Macedonian*; commodore in the Second War with the Barbary Pirates with James Madison as president when he caused the Bey of Algiers to sue for peace. In 1816, Decatur moved to Washington where he became a member of the Board of Naval Commissioners, built his still extant house on Lafayette Square in 1818 designed by Benjamin Henry Latrobe and was killed in a duel in 1820 by a fellow U.S. Naval officer.

Samuel Francis DuPont was born in 1803 to Victor Marie du Pont on the family estate in what is now Bayonne, New Jersey. His uncle (and future father-in-law) Eleuthere Irenee du Pont was the founder of E.I. du Pont de Nemours Company. Young Samuel was appointed in 1815 a midshipman in the U.S. Navy. He contributed to the conquest of California during the Mexican War. He also aided in the transformation of the navy to steam-powered ships and helped establish the curriculum for the new naval academy.

At the start of the Civil War, after his design of the blockade as head of the "Blockade Board," Du Pont was appointed commander of the South Atlantic Blockading Squadron. In recognition of his capture of Port Royal in South Carolina in 1862, he was promoted to rear admiral. Having failed to capture Charleston Harbor in the spring of 1863, he retired with an undeserved stain on his reputation.

David Farragut was born in western North Carolina in 1801. After his father's death, he was adopted by the naval officer David Porter, a family friend. He went to sea as a midshipman in 1810 and fought under his adoptive father in the War of 1812. He was made lieutenant in 1822 and captain in 1855. Suspect because of his southern origin, he was vouchsafed by his foster brother Daniel Dixon Porter. In command of the Gulf Blockading Squadron, he captured the highly important city of New Orleans in April 1862. Promoted to the newly created rank of rear admiral for his exploit, he was also associated with Ulysses Grant in the Vicksburg campaign. He is particularly noted for his capture of Mobile Bay in August 1864 for which he was promoted to the newly established rank of vice-admiral and then once again to the newly created rank of admiral in 1866.

Horatio Gates was born in 1728 in Deptford England. Commissioned in the British Army, he fought in the War of Austrian Succession in the 1740s and in the Seven Years War, particularly under General Edward Braddock in his unsuccessful expedition to the site of present day Pittsburgh. Moving to Virginia, he joined the Continental Army at the start of the American Revolution. Because of his extensive administrative experience, he was appointed the first Adjutant-General of the Continental Army. He considered himself to be more qualified than George Washington to lead the Continental Army but the plan to place him in command by some of Washingt0n's officers was aborted.

In command of the Northern Army, he is credited with the victory over General Burgoyne at Saratoga in 1777. He did poorly in command in the South and was relieved after the disastrous Battle of Camden in South Carolina in 1778.

Nathanael Greene was born in Warwick Rhode Island in 1742. Self-taught, he was aided in his education by Reverend Ezra Stiles, later president of Yale. Starting in 1775 as a private in the Rhode Island Volunteers, he became commander of these troops in the Continental Army and fought at New York and the Battle of Monmouth before taking command in 1780 in the South to replace Gates. Greene was successful there at a series of battles against Cornwallis starting at Kings Mountain ending at Guildford Courthouse that brought the British withdrawal to Yorktown and their eventual defeat.

Oliver Howard was born in Leeds Maine in 1830. After study at Bowdoin College in Brunswick Maine, he graduated from West Point in 1854. His conversion to evangelical Christianity while on duty in the Seminole War had a major influence on his future life. Colonel of the 3rd Maine Regiment at the start of the Civil War, he became brigade commander in the Peninsular Campaign with the loss of his right arm at the Battle of Fair Oaks. At Antietam, Chancellorsville and then Gettysburg, he was division and then corps commander without distinguishing himself. Transferred to the Western theater, he took part in the Battle of Missionary Ridge that won control of Chattanooga in November 1863. Upon the death of General James McPherson near Atlanta, Howard was appointed commander of the Army of the Tennessee, replacing the temporarily appointed General John A. Logan.

Moreover, Howard is most famous for his role as Commissioner of the Freedmen's Bureau from 1865 to 1874. His organization provided support for those freed including most importantly the building of churches and schools. One of the latter was his namesake Howard University in Washington DC that became the centerpiece of the Black university system. Freedman's Hospital (the forerunner of present day Howard University Hospital) at 6th Street and Boundary Road (Florida Avenue) was also established nearby in the area of the former Campbell Hospital used during the Civil War.

The selection of Mordecai Johnson as its first Negro president in 1926 was a milestone in the development of Howard University. During the 1930s, Johnson brought there the cream of the leading Negro scholars in an attempt to create a first-rate albeit segregated university. Despite its chronic financial and administrative crises, Howard University was an important base for the development and maintenance of a black professional class in Washington. It also had the best physical plant of any of the black colleges and was situated in the middle of the wealthiest and most intellectually engaged Negro community in the nation. The Founders' Library in the neo-Georgian style of the 1930s is but one example of the improvements on the Howard campus during his tenure.

In 1929, Charles Hamilton Houston became the new dean of the Howard University Law School. A graduate of Amherst and Harvard Law School, he used the law school where budding lawyers would be trained to overcome segregation. Graduating first in his class, Thurgood Marshall was hired in 1936 by his former teacher to join the NCAAP Legal Defense Fund to litigate against segregated schools.

The issue of the education of black children in the South was central to the entire history of slavery. Education had been denied to blacks during slavery. After Emancipation, the Freedman's Bureau had as its greatest accomplishment, against heavy resistance, the building of thousands of schools for Black children throughout the South. During the brief period of Reconstruction, public schools, segregated as they were, first received tax money. With the disenfranchisement of Blacks in the post-Reconstruction era, Southern tax monies that were never plentiful did not find their way to improve schools for black children. The inadequate schools made literacy tests a useful way to disenfranchise Black voters. The principle of "separate but equal" enshrined in the 1896 Supreme Court decision of Plessey vs Ferguson applied universally, in education as well as in public conveyances. The dual educational system of the South was clearly both separate and unequal.

The National Association for the Advancement of Colored People (NAACP) hired its first lawyer in 1915 to use the law courts to challenge segregation. Finally, after World War II, the cases were first argued for admission to law schools as a less threatening issue than lower grades in the public schools. In 1948, Thurgood Marshall won a case re the University of Oklahoma Law School that "equality, even in regard to physical facilities, never can be achieved...the terms...'separate' and 'equal' can not be used...there can be no separate equality." In 1950, the effort by the University of Oklahoma to place a Black student in an anteroom outside a classroom and be given separate tables in the library etc was struck down. The time had come to challenge openly segregation in public schools.

In a unanimous opinion to the credit of the still new Chief Justice Earl Warren, the Supreme Court in 1954 stripped legitimacy from racial segregation in American public education. The famous *Brown vs Topeka Board of Education* decision was raised by the Legal Defense Fund that included Thurgood Marshall and the team from Howard University. The Court ruled that "separate educational facilities are inherently unequal" in violation of the "equal protection" clause of the 14th Amendment. School desegregation was initiated in 1954 but proceeded "with all deliberate speed" over the next 20 years while Thurgood Marshall became the first Black to be appointed a Supreme Court Justice in the 1960s under President Lyndon Johnson.

Stephen W. Kearny was born in 1794 in Newark New Jersey. He went to public school and then Columbia College before joining the New York militia. A lieutenant in the War of 1812, he remained in the U.S. Army for the rest of his life. He was the foremost ante-bellum military leader on the western American frontier. In the 1830s, he founded the forerunner of the U.S. Cavalry; in the 1840s, he protected emigrants along the Oregon Trail from marauding Indians. During the Mexican War, he conquered New Mexico before carrying out an extraordinary overland expedition that helped secure Alta California.

Henry Knox was born in Boston in 1750. Forced to leave the Boston Latin School due to the death of his father, he was self-educated in his role as a bookseller in Boston. Active in the militia, he joined the Continental Army in Boston in 1775. He is credited with setting up the artillery that forced the British to evacuate Boston in 1776. Fighting with the Continental Army in various campaigns, he particularly distinguished himself at the Battle of Monmouth New Jersey in July 1778. Appointed Secretary of War by President George Washington, he helped create the army to fight in the Indian wars in the Northwest Territory.

Gilbert Marquis de Lafayette, born in 1757 in Auvergne to an aristocratic family was known as Gilbert du Motier, Marquis de Lafayette. He joined the French Army at age 16, and then volunteered for the Continental Army in 1776 under the auspices of Benjamin Franklin, then envoy to France. Young Lafayette was aide-de-camp to General Washington and was wounded at the Battle of Brandywine in 1777. He returned to France to secure aid for the colonists before taking part in the final Battle of Yorktown in 1781. An honorary American citizen, he made a triumphal tour of the United States in 1824 when the President's Park facing the White House was named after him.

James Lawrence was born in 1781 in Burlington New Jersey. His father, a Loyalist, moved to Britain leaving him in the care of a half-sister. He entered the U.S. Navy as a midshipman in 1798. Active in the "Quasi-War" with France and the First Barbary Pirates War, he was second-in-command under Stephan Decatur in the capture of the *USS Philadelphia* in the harbor of Tripoli. During the War of 1812, as the captain of the 50-gun frigate *USS Chesapeake*, he met the challenge offered by the commander of the *HMS Shannon* and was mortally wounded in the battle in June 1813. His exhortation of "Don't give Up the Ship" became the motto of his namesake ship in the victory in the Battle of Lake Erie under the command of his close friend Oliver Hazard Perry that following September.

John A Logan was born in 1826 in Murphysboro in southern Illinois. Unschooled until age fourteen, he went to Shiloh College, fought in the Mexican War and graduated from the Law Department at the University of Louisville in 1851. He was elected to the U.S. Congress as a **Stephen Douglas** Democrat in 1858 and 1860. He resigned to command the 31st Illinois Volunteer Regiment, became a brigade and then corps commander under **General James B. McPherson**. After the latter's death in July 1864, Logan received only a temporary appointment as commander of the Army of the Tennessee. The most effective of the "political generals," he was nevertheless distrusted by those trained at West Point and denied permanent command.

The issue of the volunteer citizen-soldier versus the professional soldier became one of his lasting concerns as commander of the Grand Army of the Republic (GAR), the veteran's organization. He was re-elected to the Congress from 1867 to 1871; and to the U.S. Senate from 1871 to 1888. He was the unsuccessful Republican candidate for vice-president with James Blaine in 1884, losing to **Grover Cleveland**.

Douglas MacArthur was born in 1880 the son of General Arthur MacArthur, the hero of the Battle of Missionary Ridge at Chattanooga in December 1863. He grew up on a series of army posts in the American West, was first in his class at West Point in 1903, chief of staff of the 42nd Rainbow Division during World War I and finally Major General and Chief of Staff of the U.S. Army in 1930. In that last role, he was responsible for the forcible removal in July 1932 from the Anacostia tidal flats of the World War I veterans seeking a bonus.

He retired from the U.S. Army in 1937 to serve as Field Marshal in the Philippine Army. Reactivated in 1941, he was Commander U.S. Army Far East when his air force was destroyed on the ground on December 8th 1941. He was eventually forced to abandon his troops on Bataan to become Supreme Commander Southwest Pacific headquartered in Australia. He led his forces back to the Philippines and eventually took the surrender of the Japanese in August 1945 following the use of atomic bombs on Hiroshima and Nagasaki. Post war ruler of Japan, MacArthur maintained the existence of an emperor while creating a more democratic constitution.

With the invasion of South Korea by North Korea across the 38th Parallel in June 1950, MacArthur became Supreme Commander of the U.N. sponsored force in Korea. In a desperate situation, limited only to control of a small area at the tip of the Korean peninsula, he outflanked the North Koreans by carrying out a successful landing at Inchon near the 38th Parallel. He failed to predict the entry of Chinese forces following his subsequent invasion of North Korea. The Americans were forced to retreat with heavy losses during the winter of 1951. The use of nuclear bombs was discussed but not implemented due to concern that MacArthur could not be trusted. Once again regaining control of the territory of South Korea, MacArthur sought a more complete victory with the conquest of North Korea; he disputed plans by President Harry Truman to try to negotiate an armistice. Trying to enlist political support in the Congress for his position, he was forced to resign. He was met with a tumultuous welcome but was never reinstated and the threat of Ceasarism averted.

Alexander Macomb was born in the then frontier Detroit in 1782. Macomb County is the name given to the area immediately north of Detroit's Wayne County. A hero in the War of 1812, a gold medal was ordered struck by Congress for Macomb's victory over a far larger British force at the Battle of Plattsburgh New York near Lake Champlain in September 1814. He was appointed Commanding General of the U.S. Army in 1828 by President John Quincy Adams. The choice of Macomb, an engineer rather than a line officer, was due to the conflict over seniority of the two competing more likely candidates. Army Commander during the Jackson Administration, his wife was involved in the controversy by the cabinet wives of Washington concerning the social acceptance of Peggy O'Neale Eaton, the wife of then Secretary of War. Winfield Scott succeeded him in 1841.

James B. McPherson was born near Norwalk Ohio in 1828. A classmate of Phillip Sheridan and John Bell Hood, he graduated first in his class at West Point in 1853. Appointed to the Corps of Engineers, he was Chief of Engineers with General Ulysses Grant at Fort Henry and Fort Donaldson in February 1862, Brigadier General after Shiloh, Corps Commander in the Army of the Tennessee. He became its commander in the spring of 1864 following the elevation of General Grant to U.S. Army Commanding General and William T. Sherman to overall commander in the West. McPherson was killed during July 1864 during the Atlanta Campaign by forces under the command of his old friend John Bell Hood.

Montgomery Meigs was born in 1816 in Augusta Georgia to a family native to Philadelphia where he then grew up. He graduated West Point in 1836. From 1852 to 1860, he built the Washington Aqueduct while simultaneously overseeing the building of the U.S. Capitol Extension. Appointed Brigadier General and Quartermaster General, he succeeded in meeting the extraordinary supply needs of Union Army. A staunch Unionist, he insured that the Lee family could never return to Arlington House that became after 1864 the Arlington National Cemetery. After the war, he continued to supervise construction of several important Washington buildings including the National Museum (now the Art and Industries Building of the Smithsonian) and the Federal Pension Bureau.

Samuel Nicholson (John Nicholson) were brothers born in Chestertown Maryland in the 1730s. They were both naval captains during the Revolutionary War. Samuel was also the first commander of the *USS Constitution* (Old Ironsides). John, the senior captain and then commodore in the U.S. Navy, had a less distinguished career.

Edward O.C. Ord was born in Cumberland Maryland in 1818. He graduated from West Point in 1839 with his roommate William T. Sherman.

Assigned to the artillery, he fought in the Second Seminole War before going to Monterey in 1847 along with Sherman. He built the Presidio there and surveyed both the cities of Sacramento and Los Angeles. During the Civil War, he became a corps commander at Vicksburg. The commander of the Army of the James, he helped bring about the surrender of Robert E. Lee at Appomattox Courthouse in April 1865.

Oliver Hazard Perry was born in 1785 in South Kingston Rhode Island, the son of a naval captain. He became a midshipman in 1799 under the command of his father. During the War of 1812, he commanded the naval forces on Lake Erie. He won several battles with the most famous the Battle of Lake Erie in September 1813, crucial to American success in safeguarding the Ohio Valley. The motto "Don't Give Up the Ship" was associated with his flagship in that battle, the *USS Lawrence*, named after his close friend who had just died in battle with that phrase on his lips.

Daniel Dixon Porter was born in 1813 to a family closely identified with the history of the U.S. Navy. The original David Porter, born in Boston in 1780, commanded a ship during the Revolution. His son, Commodore David Porter retired to Washington after the War with the Barbary Pirates. With his prize money, he purchased a property atop Meridian Hill. Called by him "Mount Pleasant," the name was later given to this entire area when it was subdivided after the Civil War. His house, bought by the fledgling Columbian College (later George Washington University), became a hospital during the Civil War before it burned down.

One of five naval officer brothers, Daniel Dixon Porter first went to sea as a midshipman when age ten. He was prone to act rashly but confidently. An example was his plan, in April 1861, to act directly to relieve Fort Pickens in Florida. On his own, to the detriment of both plans, he assigned himself command of a crucial ship, which Secretary of the Navy Welles had assigned to relieve Fort Sumter. Because of his reputation of energetic action, Lincoln supported his command at Vicksburg that ended successfully in July 1863 with its capture. He had less success in the Red River expedition to Shreveport in Louisiana in the spring of 1864. Nevertheless, he ended the war as a Vice-Admiral just below his foster brother Admiral David Farragut.

John A. Rawlins was born in Galena Illinois in 1831. At the outbreak of war in 1861, he joined with Ulysses S Grant in raising a regiment from that area. Serving as chief-of-staff, Rawlins remained with Grant throughout the war as the latter rose in rank and responsibility. When elected president, Grant appointed him his first Secretary of War. He held that office for the short time remaining before his death from tuberculosis.

Jesse Reno was born in Wheeling (then in Virginia) in 1823. His name is an Anglicized version of the original French "Renault." He graduated from West Point in 1846. Assigned to the artillery, he was cited for bravery while fighting under General Winfield Scott at the Battle of Chapultepec at Mexico City. He taught mathematics at the West Point military academy and commanded several arsenals before becoming a brigade and then corps commander in the Army of the Potomac. He was killed on September 12, 1862 while leading his troops at the Battle of South Mountain.

Thomas J. Rodman is still another military man during the Civil War. Graduated from West Point in 1841, he was assigned to the U.S. Army Ordnance Department where he spent his entire career. The "Rodman gun" he invented was far larger than previous cast-iron cannon and was also a far more reliable and stronger weapon. His new "wet chill" method involved casting around a hollow core while cooling the inside of the barrel. The huge guns he was able to make, as large as 15-inch bore, were primarily used for permanent fixed positions such as in the circle of forts protecting Washington. There is a picture of one of these huge guns being pulled by a mule train through the streets of Washington on the historical kiosk at the northwest corner of 15th Street and Pennsylvania Avenue. Seldom fired in anger, they remained the primary coast defense American weapons throughout the last half of the 19th century.

Winfield Scott was born in 1786 on the family plantation in Dinwiddie County near Petersburg Virginia. Commissioned in 1808, he was promoted to Brigadier General during the War of 1812 for his leadership of his disciplined troops in a series of battles on the Niagara Frontier in 1814. After the war, he was the author of the first U.S. Army drill regulations and acquired his nickname of "Old Fuss and Feathers" for his strictness so disliked by his militia soldiers. He became Commanding General of the U.S. Army in 1841. His greatest success in the Mexican War was the capture of Mexico City following the route of Cortez after landing at Vera Cruz. After the war, he was the unsuccessful Whig presidential candidate in 1852. Still Commanding General at the outbreak of the Civil War, he remained loyal to the Union, insured the safety of President Lincoln at his inauguration and counseled that the war would be a long one to be won by a blockade and the capture of the Mississippi River. Denigrated as merely an "Anaconda" strategy, it proved to be accurate. He retired in the fall of 1861 after the failure at the 1st Battle of Bull Run under his appointee General McDowell and the appointment of George McClellan as his successor.

John Sedgwick was the highest ranking Union casualty in the Civil War. Born in Connecticut, he graduated from West Point in 1837. Fighting in the Mexican War, he was promoted to brevet major. A division commander in the Army of the Potomac, he fought in the Peninsular Campaign and at

Antietam, where he was severely injured. A corps commander at Chancellorsville, he remained in that role at the Battle of the Wilderness in the Overland Campaign of 1864. He was killed by a Confederate sharpshooter from a great distance on the front lines on the morning of the day of the Battle of Spotsylvania on May 9, 1864.

Philip Sheridan was born in 1831 to Irish immigrant parents and grew up in Somerset, Ohio. Just five feet, five inches tall, he was famously described by Lincoln as "a brown, chunky little chap…and with such long arms that if his ankles itch he can scratch them without stooping." He graduated from West Point in 1848 but did not see action in the Mexican War. An infantry lieutenant assigned to the Western Theatre at the start of the Civil War, he was eventually given a cavalry command in 1862. His aggressiveness led to his promotion to major general by April 1863. As part of the Army of the Cumberland, he distinguished himself at the Battle of Chattanooga in November 1863. Scorning danger, he led the charge up Missionary Ridge on foot.

Brought to the Eastern Theatre, Sheridan was given command of the Cavalry Corps of the Army of the Potomac. His activities as commander of the Army of the Shenandoah starting in August 1864 ensured his reputation. The goal was not only to destroy the army of Jubal Early but also to deprive the capital of the Confederacy at Richmond of what had been its breadbasket. He did so by instituting a "scorched earth" policy to burn the local harvest. Sheridan had created the model for the activities carried out later that fall by General Sherman in Georgia in his March to the Sea. On October 19, 1864,

Sheridan succeeded in his other goal by rallying his troops from what appeared to be a Confederate victory at Cedar Creek; the action became the basis for his statue at Sheridan Circle and his promotion to major general. This victory also aided Abraham Lincoln's crucial reelection in November 1864. In the spring of 1865, Sheridan's victory at Saylor's Creek on April 6 was instrumental in bringing Lee to surrender at Appomattox on April 12.

In 1867, President Ulysses Grant appointed Sheridan to the command of the Department of the Missouri to pacify the Plains Indians. He followed the policy he had used in the Shenandoah Valley by depriving the Indians of their source of food by killing the bison herds by the million. By the 1880s, Sheridan had become the commanding general of the U.S. Army. As if to redeem his actions in the destruction of the bison, in 1883 he persuaded President Chester Arthur to rescind the award to railroad interests of large parts of the Yellowstone River Basin. Placed by him under military control, Yellowstone remained free of development and a refuge for wildlife, including bison, until the formation of Yellowstone National Park under the National Park Service in 1916.

William Tecumseh Sherman was born in Ohio. Near the top of his class at West Point, he remained in the Army until 1853. At the start of the war, he was teaching at a military school in Louisiana that later became Louisiana State University. Although offered a commission by the Confederates, he joined the Union. After service at Vicksburg, he was appointed by his friend General Ulysses Grant as his successor as commander of the Army of Tennessee. Sherman then carried out the famous March to the Sea through Georgia. After Grant became president in 1868, Sherman succeeded him as commander of the U.S. Army; less interested in supporting Negro rights, he was more reluctant than Grant to involve the U.S. Army in the Reconstruction of the South.

George Thomas was born in Southampton County in southeastern Virginia in 1816 on a large slave holding farm. He is credited with teaching his family slaves to read and write. He graduated from West Point in 1840, a roommate of William T. Sherman. Twelfth in class standing, he was assigned to the artillery. Braxton Bragg, later his principal antagonist in the Civil War, was his commander in the army of **Zachary Taylor** on the Texas border. Holding the line at Buena Vista (where **Jefferson Davis'** Mississippi regiment saved the day), he was promoted to brevet major. To his embarrassment, he was given a ceremonial sword by his neighbors in Southampton County in recognition of his feats. This was later deposited by his unreconstructed Confederate family in the Southern Historical Society.

After the Mexican war, he was assigned to West Point as an instructor in artillery and cavalry. With the assistance of then Academy Superintendant Robert E Lee, he was able to reorganize his department and acquire the necessary horses. In recognition of his record in Mexico, Jefferson Davis, then Secretary of War, promoted Thomas in 1855 to be major in the newly formed 2nd Cavalry Regiment under the command of Robert E Lee.

His family in Virginia felt that he had departed from his own people after his marriage to a woman from Troy New York. After the secession of his native state, Thomas remained in the U.S. Army along with his mentor General Winfield Scott. A lone southerner, he was also, in the absence of the Virginia delegation in the Congress, without political influence in his behalf.

Made a brigade commander, he reorganized the Kentucky volunteers into the First Kentucky Brigade, the nucleus of what became the Army of the Cumberland. He remained in the western theater throughout the war. In January 1862 at Mill Springs, Thomas achieved the first Union victory in the war and reclaimed eastern Kentucky based on his superior leadership against a larger Confederate force. Having invaded Kentucky in the summer of 1862, the Confederate Generals Braxton Bragg and Kirby Smith were forced to withdraw by Thomas after the Battle of Perryville in October 1862. One of three corps commanders under Rosecrans in the Army of the Cumberland, in response to the continual harassment by Confederate raids on the railroad lines, Thomas organized pioneer crews using pre-fabricated bridge trusses to repair lines.

On the eve of 1863, he was instrumental in achieving victory at the Battle of Murfreesboro (Stone's River). During the spring and summer of 1863, the Army of the Cumberland under Rosecrans and Thomas managed to maneuver Bragg entirely out of Tennessee culminating in the capture of the crucial railroad center of Chattanooga in September 1863. The armies met at Chickamauga soon after when Thomas maintained the left wing of the army throughout the day as its other wings collapsed, earning the nickname of the "Rock of Chickamauga." Finally appointed to the command of the Army of the Cumberland, his success at Missionary Ridge was important in lifting the siege of Chattanooga in November 1863. With Sherman now overall commander in the west, Thomas was responsible for maintaining supplies from his depot in Nashville for 100,000 men over 600 miles of track in support of the Atlanta campaign.

In the meantime, in accordance with the wishes of Lincoln, six regiments of black soldiers entered the Army of the Cumberland. Unlike Sherman who refused them, Thomas accepted them as a matter of course. In the absence of Sherman intent on the pillaging expedition of the March through Georgia, and about to be relieved, Thomas destroyed John Bell Hood's Army of Tennessee at the Battle of Franklin near Nashville in December 1864. Thomas made his Army of the Cumberland the most modern of its day with his mastery of such advanced for its time technology as maps and telegraph, logistics and combination of infantry, cavalry and artillery.

Born a Southerner in the Union Army and without political sponsorship in Washington, he rose to his high rank on merit alone. Recognition of his success did not come readily from Halleck or Grant. During Reconstruction, he fought for the rights of the freedmen and against the Ku Klux Klan. Considered a traitor by his Southern family members, none was present at his funeral in 1869. Moreover, his long term reputation suffered from his relatively early death and his adamant refusal to write a self-serving memoir, an opportunity available to those generals who were longer lived.

Emory Upton was born in Batavia New York in 1839 and attended Oberlin College before graduating from West Point in 1861. Assigned to the artillery, he was wounded at 1st Battle of Bull Run, fought in the Peninsular and Maryland Campaigns before being given command of the 121st New York Regiment at Fredericksburg in December 1862. A division commander at Gettysburg, he was then particularly famous for devising a successful shock assault tactic at Spotsylvania Courthouse in May 1864.

After the war, he visited the battlefields of Europe and recommended a set of reforms in the training of the U.S. Army that had far reaching impact, comparable to that of Captain Mahan on the U.S. Navy.

Artemas Ward was born in Shrewsbury (Worcester County) Massachusetts in 1727. He graduated Harvard College in 1747. Active in local politics, he was also a leader in the militia during the French and Indian War. Elected to the Massachusetts General Court, he opposed British taxation along with Samuel Adams and James Otis. As commander of the Massachusetts militia, he was appointed major general in the Continental Army second to George Washington. After the Revolutionary War, he served in the U.S. House of Representatives from 1791 to 1795.

Joseph Warren, one of the early heroes of the American Revolution, was born in 1741 in Roxbury Massachusetts. He attended Roxbury Latin School and graduated from Harvard College in 1759 before studying medicine. He was closely associated with Samuel Adams, John Hancock and the "Sons of Liberty." Boston was the center of resistance to Britain in the 1760s leading to the closing of the port and its military occupation.

In 1773-1775, he was on the Boston Committee of Correspondence and President of the Massachusetts Provincial Congress. In this role, he was responsible for ordering both Paul Revere and William Dawes to ride through the night to warn of the raid to capture Adams at Lexington and the military stores at Concord. Warren placed himself in danger when he took part in harassing the soldiers on their return from Concord. Placing himself deliberately in even greater danger in the Battle of Bunker Hill in June 1775, he was killed and his body mutilated when recognized.

Anthony Wayne was born in Pennsylvania in 1745. He led the Pennsylvania militia and the Pennsylvania Line in the Continental Army during the Revolutionary War. He distinguished himself at the Battle of Monmouth in 1778. He was particularly successful in the capture of Stony Point in 1779. After the war, he organized and trained "The Legion of the United States" to fight in the wars against the Indians of the Northwest Territory. His victory in the Battle of Fallen Timber in northwestern Ohio in 1794 opened that area to Euro-American settlement.

CHAPTER 5
FAMOUS WRITERS, SCIENTISTS AND PHILANTHROPISTS

There are somewhat more than forty names of non-military figures and those primarily known for other than their rather fleeting political office whose names are recalled on the streets of Washington. They heavily reflect the influence of New Englanders on the cultural history of the United States during the 19th century.

Jean-Jacques (John James) Audubon was born in 1785 on his father's sugar plantation in Haiti; an illegitimate son to a family also containing half-sisters from his father's other Creole mistress. Raised in France by his father's official wife, his life was affected by the ongoing Napoleonic Wars. He came to Philadelphia in 1803 to escape conscription. He carried out various businesses in Kentucky and then Missouri before devoting himself to his early love of birds.

Starting in 1820, he began his travels throughout the South to document *The Birds of America*. His great work was sold to subscribers and published over a period of several years with hand colored copper engravings of approximately 700 birds.

Henry Bacon was born in Illinois in 1866. He trained at the University of Illinois and then travelled in Europe. He closely identified with the architect Charles McKim in his commitment to classical architecture. The design of the Lincoln Memorial as a Greek temple similar to the Parthenon attests to this commitment.

George Bancroft was born in 1800 at Worcester Massachusetts to a long-established New England family. He was educated at Phillips' Exeter Academy and Harvard College, graduating in 1817. He also trained at the University of Heidelberg and Gottingen, graduating with a doctorate from the latter in 1820. He founded a model secondary school to exemplify his own educational experience.

He became known as a writer in the *North American Review* and published in 1834 the first volume of his highly popular massive History of the United States. Starting with "The Discovery of the North American Continent," the story is of the unfolding of God's purpose in the progress of development of American religious and political liberty. Politically active in Democratic Party politics in Massachusetts, he was appointed in 1845 as Secretary of the Navy by President James Polk. Bancroft Hall at the Annapolis Naval Academy still attests to its establishment during his tenure.

Benjamin Banneker was born in 1731 on his family farm near what became Ellicott's Mills on the Patapsco River near Baltimore. A free Black, he received schooling from a local Quaker. In 1788, aided by members of the neighboring Quaker Ellicott family, he began to study astronomy. In 1791, he worked with Andrew Ellicott in the survey of the boundary of the District of Columbia. From 1792 to 1797, he published yearly almanacs containing his predictions of solar and lunar eclipses. His reputation caused Thomas Jefferson to withdraw his statement that there was no African-American who had contributed to knowledge of science.

Clara Barton was born in Oxford Massachusetts in 1821. She discovered her life role to be a nurse when, merely eleven years old, she nursed her brother to health after a severe injury. A school teacher, she was denied, because of her gender, the executive position in a school she had founded. She moved to Washington in 1854 to respond to the opportunity offered to women for jobs in the Patent Office at pay equivalent to men but lost her job under the next presidential administration.

Returning to the Patent Office in 1860, she nursed men of the 6th Massachusetts Regiment, many originally from her area, wounded in April 1861 in their transit though Baltimore to aid in the defense of the capital city. She next found her role to bring supplies to help the wounded directly on the battlefields and later founded the Office of Missing Soldiers to identify those eligible for pensions. After the war, she became active with Susan B Anthony in the women's suffrage movement, an ongoing commitment for the rest of her life. During the Franco-Prussian War in 1871, she became involved once again with bringing help to soldiers and refugees. She then founded what in 1881 became the American Red Cross, committed to aid in civilian as well as military settings. Her home at Glen Echo Maryland remains as her memorial and the early headquarters of the Red Cross organization she founded and led until 1904.

Henry Ward Beecher was born in Litchfield Connecticut in 1813 as one of eight children of a rigorously Calvinist minister. He was particularly close to his sister Harriet Beecher Stowe, later famous for her *Uncle Tom's Cabin*. He trained at Amherst College and at a theological seminary near Cincinnati headed by his father. He became minister in 1847 of the newly formed Plymouth Congregational Church in Brooklyn Heights New York where he remained for the rest of his career.

One of the most famous preachers of his time, he was active in the anti-slavery and women's suffrage movements. Committed to reform movements, he thought that the predestination of his Calvinist antecedents did not preclude the ability of men and women to bring about improvement by removing the evils of society. Known as "The Gospel of Love," he preached that Jesus was compassionate and loved all sinners.

Alexander Graham Bell was born in 1847 in Edinburgh Scotland to a family famous for its work in the teaching of speech. Inventive and interested in science since childhood, Bell helped his mother cope with her increasing deafness by reading lips, called "Visible Speech." He attended the University of Edinburgh and then the University of London. The family immigrated in 1870 to Canada, settling at Brantford Ontario.

Bell moved to Boston in 1871 to work at the Horace Mann School for the Deaf and then the Clarke School in Northampton. He became a private tutor for Mabel Hubbard, deaf since a bout of scarlet fever at age five. His work on the "acoustic telegraph" came to the attention of his tutee's father. Gardiner Greene Hubbard sponsored his research and eventually ensured the viability of the 1876 Bell patent and the resultant telephone monopoly. After marriage to Mabel, the Bell family moved to Washington to defend the patent. Bell continued to carry on his inventions at his laboratory in the area of Volta Place in Georgetown with the phonograph and the hydrofoil one of the many patents illustrating the range of his interests.

William Cullen Bryant, born in Massachusetts in 1784 to a family of early New England background, studied at Williams College. He then trained as a lawyer but became famous as a poet for his *Thanatopsis (Meditation on Death)* published in 1817. As editor-in-chief from 1827 until 1878 of the *New York Evening Post* newspaper, he espoused a progressive viewpoint as a "Free-Soil" member of the Republican Party from the time of its origin in the 1850s. His activity as a member of the New York City community in helping to establish the New York Medical College and the Metropolitan Museum of Art is recognized by the naming of Bryant Park at 42nd Street in that city

James Bryce was born in 1838 to Scottish parents in Belfast Northern Ireland, educated at Belfast Academy, University of Glasgow and then at the University of Heidelberg and Trinity College at Oxford. A Fellow of Oriel College Oxford, he was also called to the Bar at Lincoln's Inn in 1867. Regius Professor of Civil Law at Oxford from 1870 to 1893, he was elected as a Liberal to Parliament from 1886 to 1907 and served in several Liberal Party governments. The author of *The American Commonwealth* in 1886, he became British Ambassador to the United States in 1907. Serving until 1913, he helped cement Anglo-American relations during the period leading to World War I. While living in Washington, he noted the beauty of the view from the high point at the corner of Massachusetts and Wisconsin Avenues where his namesake park now sits

Daniel Burnham was born in New York State but grew up in Chicago. Apprenticed to a draftsman, he later formed his architectural firm of Burnham & Root, noted for their early skyscrapers in the Chicago style of architecture. After the unexpected death of his partner, and now under the influence of Charles McKim, Burnham carried out the 1893 Colombian Exposition on the shores of Lake Michigan in the classical revival style. It became a model for American cities for the next generation. The chair of the McMillan Commission in 1900-1902, Burnham also designed Washington's Union Station to implement its recommendation to create a formal National Mall. His Chicago Plan in 1909 was also a model for city planning and helped create the park system of that city.

William Ellery Channing, born in Rhode Island in 1780, was the grandson of William Ellery, a signer of the Declaration of Independence. He trained at Harvard but deviated from his New England Calvinist background in becoming one of the leading proponents of Unitarianism. Its tenets, aside for the disavowal of the Trinity, included a belief in the essential goodness of humankind and the possibility of revelation through reason rather than scripture. He became an abolitionist after the model provided by the British emancipation of slaves in the 1830s. Closely associated with members of the Transcendalist movement, Unitarianism was a particularly significant factor in New England life in the 19th century.

William Wilson Corcoran was born in 1798 in Georgetown to a well-to-do merchant. He attended Georgetown College in the District of Columbia but his life was spent in business. He became one of the nation's first significant philanthropists. His wealth came from banking. He was the founder of what became Riggs and Company, the largest bank in Washington until its demise in the 21st century. Corcoran started as an employee of the Second Bank of the United States in Washington and opened his own firm when that bank was closed in 1836 by Andrew Jackson. In partnership with George Riggs, Jr in 1840, he entered the banking business as Corcoran and Riggs.

The first of the government loans guaranteed by the firm was at the time of the accession of John Tyler in 1844 after the very short presidential tenure of William Henry Harrison. Corcoran then financed the $15 million payment to Mexico in return for the cession of its territory after the end of the Mexican War. The placement of that loan with London bankers in association with the American **George Peabody** was the start of what became a very profitable international banking business. He retired from active business in the 1850s and became even wealthier due to speculation in Washington real estate.

William W. Corcoran was the most prominent resident of Lafayette Park when it was the social center of the city. Corcoran liked to be in the center of things and was able, after the end of the Civil War, once again to achieve acceptance after his return to Washington from his exile in Paris as a Confederate sympathizer. His home was considered to be "the chief rendezvous for distinguished men" for the forty years from 1849 to 1888. A long-time widower, he hosted weekly stag dinners and annual balls for Congress. He knew personally all the presidents from Andrew Jackson to Grover Cleveland who all had accounts at the bank he founded. He never held public office but politicians sought him out for his social and financial advice.

One of the first of the series of wealthy American art collectors, Corcoran began to open the gallery in his art-filled home on Lafayette Park to the public in the 1850s. His extensive art collection contained as its centerpiece *The Greek Slave* by Hiram Powers. The statue had been one of the highlights of the Great Crystal Palace Exhibition in London in 1851 (to be covered when Queen Victoria visited). A copy widely toured and was a sensation wherever shown with the proviso that groups of each sex were admitted alternately into the small gallery used for its exhibition. The nude white statue was supposed to show "the fortitude and resignation of a Christian supported by her faith in the goodness of God; leaving no room for shame." It became an icon of the abolitionist movement and a miniature copy, for example, to be found in the home of Frederick Douglass.

In addition to the Corcoran Gallery of Art, among his many other benefactions in the Washington DC area were the Oak Hill Cemetery with its Renwick-designed chapel and the Corcoran School of Science of the Columbian College (processor of George Washington University).

James Buchanan Eads was born in 1820 in Lawrenceburg Indiana and grew up in St Louis Missouri. His mother was a cousin of the future president, hence her choice of his name. Self-educated, Eads made his fortune by inventing a diving bell and other methods to salvage goods from ships that sank in the Mississippi River. At the start of the Civil War, he built at Carondelet near Saint Louis a group of ironclad gunboats that helped capture Fort Henry in February 1862 and later contributed to the Union victory at the Battle of Mobile Bay in August 1864. From 1867 to 1874, he built the Eads Bridge, the first that crossed the Mississippi at St Louis.

Andrew Ellicott was born in Bucks County Pennsylvania in 1754. His family moved to Maryland to develop in 1772 their mills at the Patapsco River Falls near Baltimore. In 1754, he was part of the surveying team that completed the western portion of the Mason-Dixon Line dividing Maryland from Pennsylvania. He then defined the western border of Pennsylvania from which longitude the Northwest Territory was later laid out. He came to the attention of men such as David Rittenhouse and Benjamin Franklin, members of the American Philosophical Society in Philadelphia. In 1791, he was appointed by George Washington to survey the boundaries of the District of Columbia; and in 1792 after the departure of Peter L'Enfant, to complete the map of the City of Washington to be engraved. He was in turn in 1803 the teacher of Meriwether Lewis in preparation for the latter's expedition surveying the Louisiana Purchase.

Edward Kennedy (Duke) Ellington was born in 1899 in the West End of Washington to parents who were both pianists and grew up in the U Street area of northwest Washington. Taught the piano from early childhood, he did not take it seriously until his late teens when he learned how to read music and earn money by playing at dances around Washington DC. One of his first gigs was at the True Reformer's Hall on U Street. He moved to New York's Harlem in the early 1920s becoming well known as leader of the "Kentucky Club" Orchestra at 49th Street and Broadway. Eventually he moved to the famous "Cotton Club" in Harlem where his radio broadcasts and records made him nationally known. In the early 1930s, he toured Europe.

Composing as well as leading successive orchestras, he was one of the most famous African-American artists of his time. The bridge that carries his name connects Calvert Street to Connecticut Avenue from 18th Street NW near his U Street neighborhood.

Ralph Waldo Emerson was born in Boston in 1803, went to the Boston Latin School and graduated from Harvard College in 1821. He later went to the Harvard Divinity School and was ordained. He left the ministry but continued to preach the rest of his life a more secular philosophy expressed in his Harvard Divinity Lecture in 1838 that questioned the divinity of Christ and the veracity of the Biblical miracles. He was not invited back to Harvard for thirty years but has recently been recognized by an eponymous Universalist-Unitarian professorship at the Divinity School.

He founded in 1836 the Transcendental Club that became the nucleus of his philosophical circle that found truth in nature. The group also included Margaret Fuller who shared with him the editorship of *The Dial*, their literary magazine from 1840 to 1844. He befriended Henry Thoreau and Nathaniel Hawthorne; and, much later, Walt Whitman. Emerson is most influential for his Essays that were published starting in the 1840s. Most notable were "Self-Reliance" and "Conduct of Life." He lectured extensively throughout his life and was considered America's leading intellectual figure.

Edward Everett was born in Boston in 1794, the son of a clergyman. He attended the Boston Latin School, Phillips' Exeter Academy and graduated from Harvard College at an early age in 1811. He later received a Ph.D. from University of Gottingen in Prussia, the first American to do so. A Professor of Greek at Harvard, he was also its President in the 1840s. Interested in the propagation of the advanced Prussian educational methods, he worked with Horace Mann in improving public education. He was well known as a public intellectual.

A member of the "National Republican Union" faction in the U.S. Congress in the 1820s and Whig Governor of Massachusetts in the 1830s, he was appointed by the Whig Party President **Millard Fillmore** to fill the seat of **Daniel Webster** as Secretary of State after the latter's death in 1852. An ardent Unionist, he was the vice-presidential candidate of the Constitution Union Party in 1860 along with John Bell of Tennessee. He is now best remembered for his Gettysburg Address where his two-hour scholarly oration pales in the light of Lincoln's own far shorter one at the same time.

Euclid is said to have lived in 300s BCE and credited with founding the field of mathematics. His *Elements* codified the work of previous mathematicians and provided a logical coherent system subject to rigorous proofs that forms the basis for the teaching of geometry even to the present day. The presence of his name on one of the streets of Washington may be credited to the Colombian College that existed in that area.

Michael Faraday was born in 1791 to poor parents in the Borough of Southwark in London. Apprenticed to a bookbinder, he was self-educated. His interest in chemistry was aroused by the public lectures given by Sir Humphrey Davy at the Royal Institution. Hired as Davy's assistant, he later developed the laws of electrolysis, discovered benzene and isolated chlorine gas. His greatest work starting in 1831 was his discovery of the induction of electricity by changing the electromagnetic field that led eventually to the electric dynamo and electric power.

Henry Foxall was born in Monmouthshire Wales in 1758 to parents who were early followers of John Wesley. A superintendant of an ironworks in Dublin Ireland, he immigrated to Philadelphia in 1797. A friend of Thomas Jefferson, he was encouraged to set up an ironworks above Georgetown in 1800. The first and the largest of the private foundries that supplied the War and Navy Departments, it produced 300 cannon and 30,000 shot each year. His foundry produced cannon during the War of 1812 including those that equipped the ships commanded by Oliver Hazard Perry on Lake Erie in his 1813 victory. A Methodist lay preacher, he founded the Foundry Methodist Church, said to be in recognition of the safety of his foundry during the British occupation of Washington in August 1814.

Benjamin Franklin was born in Boston in 1706 as the youngest son of a poor soap maker. Apprenticed as a printer to his elder brother, he escaped from an abusive situation to come to Philadelphia in 1723. He thrived there as the publisher of the *Pennsylvania Gazette* and as the author of the popular *Poor Richard's Almanac*. Active in the 1730s and 1740s in Philadelphia civic affairs, he founded many of that city's still extant major institutions including the American Philosophical Society (the first learned society), the Library Company (the first lending library) and the Pennsylvania Hospital.

After retiring from business, he devoted himself in the 1750s to scientific studies culminating in the "kite experiment" demonstrating the electrical nature of lightening that brought him international fame. Acting as an agent for several of the American colonies in London, he returned to America in 1765 after being publically humiliated in Parliament. He became in the 1760s an ardent supporter of American independence, contributing largely to the success of the American Revolution by achieving the alliance with the French while minister to Paris from 1778 to 1785. He was the elder statesman at the Philadelphia Constitutional Convention in 1787 and is rightfully considered one of the "Founding Fathers."

Robert Fulton, born in Pennsylvania in 1765, showed from childhood an interest in mechanical inventions particularly related to boats. Deciding to be an artist, he moved to Europe in 1786, first living in London under the tutelage of the American artist Benjamin West. He later moved to Paris where in the 1790s, he designed the first experimental submarine. Returning to the United States in 1806, he is recognized for having developed, along with Robert Livingston, the first commercially successful steamship service on the Hudson River.

Galen (Claudius Galenus) was born in 100s CE to a wealthy Greek architect and philosopher in Pergamum (now Bergama Turkey). Pergamum was then at its height with a library second only to Alexandria. Well educated in philosophy, he later trained in medicine under the influence of Hippocrates. He subscribed to the theory of the four "humors" with illness resulting from an excess or deficiency of one or other, a theory that prevailed under his great influence in Western medicine until the 19th century.

Moving to Rome, he was the most famous physician of his time. He remains known for his careful observations of the epidemic of what seems to be the "bubonic plague" that occurred in Rome in the 160s during the time of the Emperor Marcus Aurelius. In accordance with the tenets of

Hippocratic practice, his description of the illness focuses on the prognostic signs.

Albert A. Gallatin was born in 1761 in Geneva Switzerland to wealthy well-connected parents. In accordance with his belief in the Enlightenment, he immigrated to America in 1780, eventually settling in Philadelphia. Active in Pennsylvania politics, he was elected to Congress in 1795 where he was a leader in the Democratic-Republican Party. Opposed to the policies of the Federalist Secretary of the Treasury **Alexander Hamilton** under President George Washington, Gallatin became Secretary of the Treasury under both Presidents **Thomas Jefferson** and **James Madison** for a record fourteen years. During his tenure, he managed to reduce the national debt despite the expense of the Louisiana Purchase but had to increase the national debt in order to finance the War of 1812. After retirement, he helped found New York University in 1831 to provide education to the working and merchant classes and the American Ethnological Society to carry on his interest in American Indian languages.

Edward Miner Gallaudet was born in 1837 in Hartford Connecticut where his father had pioneered education of the deaf and blind. Young Gallaudet graduated from Trinity College in Hartford in the 1850s. Soon after, he was invited by Amos Kendall to take over the newly founded Columbian Institution for the Deaf and Blind. By 1864, it was authorized to offer a college degree, later becoming Gallaudet University (named after his father). In his long tenure, he created the field of deaf education while championing the concept of "total communication," including the use of sign language as well as oral communication.

Joseph Gales was born at Eckington in Derbyshire England in 1786. His father, a printer, was forced to emigrate due to his republican views. Gales attended University of North Carolina before coming to Washington in 1807. He joined the *National Intelligencer* newspaper making it the city's leading daily in 1813 until its demise in 1867. During the short lived occupation of Washington by Admiral Cockburn, the latter officiated in the destruction of the newspaper's presses in recognition of its "abuse of his name." In association with his brother-in-law William Seaton, they were official printers to the U.S. Congress documenting its debates. A member of the Board of Aldermen, he was elected mayor of Washington in 1827 through 1830 participating during his term in the inaugural of the C&O Canal. His estate, named after his birthplace, became an early suburb and a stop on the B&O Railroad.

Stephen Girard was born in Bordeaux France in 1750. A sea captain engaged in trade in the Caribbean, he came to Philadelphia in 1776. He was known for his civic mindedness in caring for the sick in the recurrent yellow fever epidemics in Philadelphia in the 1790s. A successful merchant; he brought his capital home from Europe in 1811 to buy the former quarters of the 1st Bank of the United States to found his own Girard Bank. With the refusal of the Federalist New Englanders to fund a war with which disagreed, his bank funded a large part of the debt of the United States Government during the War of 1812. One of the wealthiest men in American history and childless, he founded in his will the Girard College as a boarding school for orphan boys.

Charles C. Glover was born in North Carolina in 1846. He first became a clerk at the Riggs & Company Bank in 1866, its administrative head in 1873, and the president as the Riggs National Bank in 1896. Head of the District of Columbia's largest bank, he was active particularly in the 1890s in creating Rock Creek Park, the extension of Massachusetts Avenue and the Washington National Cathedral. The bridge that bears his name carries the extension of Massachusetts Avenue over Rock Creek.

Asaph Hall was born in 1829 in Goshen Connecticut. He was primarily known for his astronomical work. First at the Harvard Observatory and then, from 1862 at the U.S, Naval Observatory, with its 26 inch telescope, he discovered the two moons of Mars.

Nathaniel Hawthorne was born in 1804 in his ancestral Salem Massachusetts. He added the letter 'w" to his surname to distinguish himself from his Puritan forbearers, including a judge unrepentant for his role in the Salem witch trials. A writer since childhood, he went to Bowdoin College from 1821 to 1825. There he met Franklin Pierce as well as Henry Wadsworth Longfellow. He was a colleague and neighbor in Concord Massachusetts of fellow writers Ralph Waldo Emerson and Herman Melville. Hawthorne's greatest success was *The Scarlet Letter* written in the early 1850s. His friend President Pierce appointed him to the plum position of Consul in Liverpool from 1853 to 1857.

Curtis Hillyer was a mining lawyer and member of the "gold syndicate" of California investors who developed the Dupont Circle area starting in the 1870s. Once a borderland of workmen's shanties, the area was graded and landscaped and converted into a setting for gilded age mansions. Hillyer chose to build his own mansion at the corner of Massachusetts Avenue and Boundary Road (Florida Avenue). It was later incorporated into the even grander home of the Townshend family that remains as the Cosmos Club with the adjacent street named after the original builder.

James Hoban was born in Ireland in 1755. Raised on the estate of the Earl of Desart, he was familiar with the characteristics of Irish Georgian manor house architecture. Trained as a draftsman in Dublin, he immigrated to Philadelphia in 1785 and then to Charleston South Carolina. Introduced to

Washington on the latter's southern tour, he was favored by George Washington and won the competition for the building of the "President's House."

The model for the design of the President's House has been attributed to Leinster House, the Dublin home of the Duke of Leinster, later Ireland's Parliament House. There were similarities in plan with the large rectangular entrance hall and eleven-bay façade. There are however, several differences such as the oval "Blue Room" and the lowering of the building to two stories from the original's three. Rushed to completion, President John Adams moved in on December 1, 1800 while plaster was still drying in the East Room. Water had to be carried in pails from the well in Franklin Square five blocks away. James Hoban remained associated with the White House for the rest of his life, responsible for its rebuilding after its destruction in 1814 and later its north portico.

James Holt Ingraham was born in Portland Maine in 1809. While working as a teacher in Natchez Mississippi, he wrote stories for popular magazines under the pen name of F. Clinton Barrington.

Washington Irving was born in Manhattan as the youngest child of prosperous Scotch-Irish immigrants. Born in 1783, he was named after the recently victorious hero of the American Revolution. Starting in 1798, he visited in Tarrytown and travelled in the Catskills, the scene of his most popular stories. His first success in 1809 was his *History of New York* written by the putative Dietrich Knickerbocker. In 1819, Irving became the first American writer with an international reputation with the publication of *Sketchbook of Geoffrey Crayon, Gent.* that included the Rip Van Winkle stories. Living in Europe until 1832, he wrote in 1828 his landmark *Life and Voyages of Christopher Columbus*. In 1842, he was appointed Minister to Spain by President John Tyler. He finished his multi-volume *Life of Washington*, his namesake, just prior to his death.

Francis Scott Key was born to a leading Maryland family and trained as a lawyer under the auspices of his uncle Philip Barton Key. He is famous for writing the national anthem based on his presence at the shelling of Fort McHenry in Baltimore Harbor in August 1814. His name lives on in the Key Bridge built adjoining his home during 1808 to 1828 at 3518 M Street.

The original "Aqueduct Bridge" carried in a flume the canal boats from the C&O Canal from Georgetown to the Virginia shore and then to Alexandria starting in the 1830s. It was converted to roadway during the Civil War, The Combined canal and roadway bridge was replaced by a road bridge in the 1880s that also carried the street railways to Rosslyn. The Key Bridge was in turn its replacement after 1917.

Sidney Lanier was born in Macon Georgia in 1841. He graduated from Oglethorpe College at the outbreak of the Civil War. A captured Confederate soldier, he was imprisoned in the federal prison at Point Lookout Maryland. There he contracted the tuberculosis that caused his early death. He studied law and practiced for a time in Montgomery Alabama. He returned to his first love of music, becoming well known as a flautist in the Peabody Institute Orchestra in Baltimore. Appointed Professor of English Literature at Johns Hopkins, he was also noted for his poetry whose meter was patterned after that of musical notation. His best known poem was *The Glynn Marshes*, about the area on the coast of Georgia.

Carl Linneus was born in southern Sweden in 1707, attended the University of Lund and then the University of Uppsala where he became Professor of Botany. One of the greatest scientists of his time, he was responsible for establishing the taxonomy of plants and the bi-nominal nomenclature that has endured. The street that bears his name was associated with an early plant nursery.

Henry Wadsworth Longfellow was born in 1807 in Portland Maine to a well-established New England family. He graduated from Bowdoin College in 1825 along with his lifelong friend Nathaniel Hawthorne. After extensive European travel, he became in 1837 Professor of Modern Languages at Harvard College. The center of a literary circle, he remained there for the rest of his career, living at the famous Craigie House on Brattle Street in Cambridge.

A writer since childhood, he was the most famous poet of his time with *Paul Revere's Ride*, *The Village Blacksmith* and many others that were highly popular. To illustrate his popularity, his 75th birthday was the equivalent to a national holiday.

James Russell Lowell was born on his family estate in Cambridge Massachusetts in 1819. He graduated from Harvard College in 1838. He published his first collection of poetry in 1841, compiled while at the Harvard Law School. He advocated abolition of slavery in his early poetry strongly influenced by the beliefs of his first wife, a fellow poet. Despondent after her death, he regained his life trajectory by lecturing on the English poets at the family-sponsored Lowell Institute in Boston. He became an editor of the *Atlantic Monthly* and Professor of Languages at Harvard College. After retirement from Harvard, in the 1870s, he was appointed minister to Spain, and later to Great Britain.

Andrew Mellon was born in Pittsburgh in 1856. His father, a Scotch-Irish immigrant from Northern Ireland, was a banker and judge. After graduating from what became the University of Pittsburgh, Mellon entered an extremely successful career in business. With investments in coal, steel, coke and aluminum, he was next to Rockefeller and Ford the richest man in the United States when made secretary of the treasury in 1921. During his tenure until 1932, he pursued a policy of low taxes and reduced expenditures. With the onset of the Great Depression, both he and his policies were in disrepute. He is more positively remembered for his philanthropy in his last years that was translated into the National Gallery of Art and the art collection he helped start. His fountain lies opposite the National Gallery he had built.

Samuel F.B. Morse was born in Charlestown Massachusetts in 1791. He trained at Phillips' Academy Andover and then Yale in 1810 before going to Europe to train in art under the American artist Washington Allston. Elected to London's Royal Academy of Art in 1811, Morse pursued a career noted especially for his portraits. Especially noteworthy were his 1821 painting of *The Hall of Congress* and *The Gallery of the Louvre* while in Paris in the early 1830s.

On his trip home from Paris, he met Charles Thomas Jackson who introduced him to electromagnetism. Morse invented a means of relaying messages along a single wire and the Morse Code. After a federal subsidy was obtained, he was able to demonstrate the feasibility of long distance transmission that led to the widespread use of the electric telegraph. The value of the telegraph was confirmed during the Civil War.

Wolfgang Amadeus Mozart was born in Salzburg Austria in 1756 to a relatively well known violinist. A child prodigy, young Mozart became known throughout the fashionable courts of Europe. Once grown, he came to Vienna in 1781 determined to make his way as a "free-lance" musician rather than a flunkey in some nobleman's retinue.

Vienna was a place where music had been especially prized by its Habsburg rulers. There was an active opera musical scene with the Italian Hof Theater and the German Singspiel. There were literally dozens of aristocratic families that competed in their support of music. Many presented concerts in their palatial quarters on a regular basis from the large pool of amateur and professional musicians. The middle class was also active in sponsoring such events. Outdoor concerts also took place in the public parks.

As the first "free-lance" composer, Mozart was required to compose for a broad public from all social levels rather than merely depend on the largess of the nobility and the court. Although he worked hard, was very prolific and wrote to meet the varied needs of different players, composing even his popular operas did not bring in much income. His major sources of funds were occasional commissions and sale of tickets to his concerts, the last very variable. The writing and performing of his own piano concertos was Mozart's vehicle for public recognition. Aside from composition, his profession was as a soloist for his many public or subscription concerts. His sonatas for piano and violin gave the piano equal prominence with the violin. His later concertos are longer, with the piano and the orchestra partners, rather than rivals.

Mozart lived in Vienna until his death in 1791, with excursions to Prague where he was better received. 1784 was a year in which he excelled as a piano soloist and in composing piano sonatas. There were six concertos in that year alone and six more during the next two years. During the especially prolific six months between October 1785 and April 1786, he composed *The Marriage of Figaro*, appeared in seven concerts, and composed three piano concertos, a violin sonata as well as numerous other pieces as inserts for operas. Invited to Prague after the success of the *Marriage of Figaro*, he did particularly well there in 1787, receiving a commission for *Don Giovanni*. On the whole, Mozart earned considerably more than most musicians with an income commensurate with that of a rather high official of the court. Although pressed for funds in 1788-1789, he was far from poor and could count on a rising income in his later years belying the romantic image of the starving composer.

Isaac Newton was born on his family's Woolthorpe Manor in Lincolnshire in 1642. He studied at Trinity College Cambridge and later became a Fellow of that college and Lucasian Professor of Mathematics. His prolific early work in the 1660s encompassed the calculus, the refraction of white light into its component colors, and the invention of the reflecting telescope. In the late 1670s, he returned to his early work on gravity to publish in 1684 his *Principia* and the famous Newtonian Laws of Universal Motion. His work defined the science of physics and astronomy until the work of Einstein in the 20th century.

James Edward Oglethorpe was born to aristocratic parents on the family estate in Surrey England in 1696. He went to Corpus Christi College at Oxford. Under the auspices of John Churchill, the 1st Duke of Marlborough, Oglethorpe became an aide-de-camp to Prince Eugene of Savoy in the Austro-Turkish War of 1716-1718. He had an intermittent military career in the wars of the 18th century including the suppression of the Jacobite Rebellion of 1745.

He is primarily noted for his philanthropic interests in behalf of imprisoned debtors. He founded the colony of Georgia with the settlement of Savannah in 1733 as a buffer to protect the English settlements against the Spanish in Florida. His plan was to create a colony in which there would equality with limited land holdings and absence of slavery. He welcomed Jewish as well as the full range of dissenting Protestant settlers.

Carlile P. Patterson was born in Mississippi in 1816 the son of a naval commodore. He became a midshipman in 1830 before training as a civil engineer at Georgetown College in Kentucky. His marriage to Elizabeth Pearson brought him ownership of Brentwood, a hundred acre property with a neo-classical mansion of that name designed in 1817 by Benjamin Henry Latrobe. Known then as the Patterson House, it was a Washington social center during the Grant Administration.

Patterson had been a longtime friend of Ulysses Grant. Patterson's sister was married to Daniel Dixon Porter, an admiral in the Civil War; another admiral brother was in charge of the Washington Navy Yard in the 1870s. Patterson was a member of the staff of the U.S. Coast Survey when he was appointed its fourth Superintendent in 1874. During his tenure, considered the Golden Age of that agency, its name was changed to the U.S. Coast and Geodetic Survey to reflect its actual activities.

George Peabody was born as one of eight children in a poor family in 1796 in what was then called South Danvers Massachusetts (now called Peabody after its favorite son). He entered the dry goods business in Baltimore in 1817 before moving to London in 1837. There he entered the banking business in association with Junius Spencer Morgan (the father of John Pierpont Morgan). Another colleague was William W. Corcoran in Washington. They specialized in the selling of American securities to British investors including U.S. Government bonds and railroad securities.

A bachelor, he used his large fortune to endow mainly educational institutions in the United States such as the Peabody School for Teachers at Vanderbilt University in Nashville Tennessee and the Peabody Institute at Johns Hopkins University in Baltimore. His philanthropy in England was devoted mainly to funding housing for the poor of London.

Isaac Pierce (Peirce), a Quaker, migrated from Chester County near Philadelphia in the 1780s. In recognition of his large land holdings, he was appointed in 1802 by President Jefferson to the Levy Court. It acted as the Board of Commissioners of the County of Washington, the area of the District of Columbia not included in the L'Enfant Plan of the City of Washington. Peirce expanded his holdings along Rock Creek with the still extant stone mill, built in 1829 of local stone quarried on Peirce property further north along Rock Creek. The major early street traversing Rock Creek was Peirce Mill Road (now Park Road to the east and Tilden Street to the west).

George Washington Riggs was born in Georgetown DC in 1813. He grew up in Baltimore where his father Elisha was a partner of George Peabody. In 1840, he joined with William W. Corcoran to form the highly successful Corcoran & Riggs Bank in Washington DC. The bank known as

Riggs & Company and then Riggs National Bank continued as Washington's largest until its demise in 2005.

David Rittenhouse was born in 1732 in Germantown Pennsylvania adjacent to Philadelphia. His entire career was associated with that city. Self-taught, he was interested from childhood in the building of working mechanical models. He exchanged one of his orreries showing the actions of the planets for a scholarship to Rutgers. He was particularly noted for his work in astronomy and was Professor of Astronomy at the University of Pennsylvania. He built the first American telescope and founded the American Astronomical Society. His greatest feat was the observation of the Transit of Venus on June 3, 1769 that enabled him to measure the distance of the Earth from the Sun as 93 million miles. A Fellow of the Royal Society in London, he succeeded Benjamin Franklin as President of the American Philosophical Society and was the greatest American scientist of his age.

John Philip Sousa was born in 1854 in the area of Washington then called "Navy Yard." He grew up at 7th and E Streets SE where his father was a trombonist in the Marine Band. Surrounded by martial music during his boyhood during the Civil War, he always recalled the joy of experiencing the May 1865 Grand Review on Pennsylvania Avenue. He was also enrolled in the Marine Band at age 12 as an apprentice musician. By the 1870s, he was playing the violin professionally, composing and conducting theater orchestras in Washington. During the 1876 Philadelphia Centennial, he played in the first violin section of the official Centennial orchestra.

He was appointed the conductor of the U.S. Marine Band in 1880. Along with the usual marches, many written by Sousa, the Band branched out to present symphonic music. In 1888, Sousa composed "Semper Fidelis", the official song of the Marine Corps. In 1889, his very popular "Washington Post March" made both him and the newspaper that commissioned it famous. He had become the "March King" just as the Viennese Johann Strauss was the "Waltz King." The greatest of his marches was the "Stars and Stripes Forever" composed in its entirety as he paced the deck on his ship in November 1896 while returning home from Europe. Sousa was then at the height of his powers having just composed *El Capitan*, the most successful of his operettas. The time, leading up to the Spanish-American War, was one of intense nationalism.

In 1890, the Columbia Phonograph Company chose to record the Marine Band in the new medium. Soon after, with the support of Mrs. Benjamin Harrison, the president's wife, he was able to tour with the Band. It had become known as America's premier military band on par with those in Europe. Having left the Navy his own Sousa Band toured the country from 1892 annually for the next thirty-nine years. There were long term engagements during the summer at such resorts as Manhattan Beach, Coney Island and Atlantic City. He went on several European tours during the decade starting in 1900. During World War I, commissioned a naval officer for the first time, he proudly led a much augmented Navy Band that raised money for Liberty Bonds.

Oscar Strauss was born in 1850 in Ottenberg Germany. His family immigrated, first to Georgia and then, after the Civil War to New York City. He graduated from Columbia College in 1871 and its Law School in 1873. After practicing law, he was associated with the family business of R.H. Macy Company. He was recurrently Minister to the Ottoman Empire in the 1889s and 1890s and then Ambassador in 1908-1910. President Theodore Roosevelt appointed him Secretary of Commerce and Labor in 1906, the first Jew to serve in the cabinet. The fountain named for him is sited in front of the International Trade Center building on 12th Street.

Alfred Lord Tennyson was born in 1809 the son of a comfortably well-off rector in Lincolnshire England. He wrote poetry from childhood and attended Trinity College Cambridge in 1827. His first published works starting in the 1830s brought him to the attention of the poet Samuel Taylor Coleridge. In 1850, his masterpiece dedicated to the memory of his close friend *In Memoriam A.H.H.* brought him to the attention of Queen Victoria. He was appointed Poet Laureate to succeed William Wordsworth and remained so for a record breaking 42 years. In 1884, he was the first writer raised to the peerage under William Gladstone and is immortalized in Westminster Abbey. His most famous poem *Charge of the Light Brigade* illustrates his skill in the use of imagery and meter.

Edward G. Tuckerman was born in Boston in 1821 to a distinguished family. He attended Harvard for a time and its law school before retiring to the life of a gentleman botanist in central Massachusetts. Reclusive, he was similar in his poetry to the neighboring Emily Dickinson but they were unknown to each other. His only published book in 1860 called *Poems* was well received by his literary friends but did not receive recognition by others.

Alessandro Volta was born in 1745 in Como Italy. In 1774, he became Professor of Physics at the Royal School in Como. In 1778, he isolated the gas methane from the waters of Lake Maggiore. He discovered the unit of electrical potential, henceforth called the "volt." From 1779, Professor at the University of Pavia, he began the research that led to the further development of Galvani's discovery of "animal electricity" and to the creation of the electric battery. The Volta Bureau established on 35th Street in Georgetown by Alexander Graham Bell follows the design of the Volta

Temple erected in his honor on the shores of Lake Como and gave its name to the street that lies alongside.

Raoul Wallenberg was born to one of Sweden's leading industrial and banking families in Stockholm in 1912. Highly educated, he travelled widely. He was assigned in 1944 to the embassy in Budapest Hungary of his neutral country. Using his diplomatic status, he provided Swedish identity cards and safe houses to protect thousands of Hungarian Jews from deportation to the death camps. Imprisoned in 1945 by the Soviet Russians, he was considered to be an American spy and never released.

John Greenleaf Whittier was born in 1807 on the family farm in Haverhill Massachusetts. His father's Quaker faith was the foundation of Whittier's strong Abolitionist commitment. William Lloyd Garrison was an early influence. They differed when Whittier moved into the political arena with the formation in the 1840s of the Liberty Party, later the Free-Soil Party. Much of his early poetry dealing with slavery was published in the *National Era* newspaper he edited. Most known was the poem *The Song of the Negro Boatmen* dealing with the freeing of the slaves at Port Royal North Carolina in 1862 during the Civil War. After the 13th Amendment and Emancipation, his writing turned to his well-known *Snowbound* and patriotic poems such as *Barbara Fretchie*.

Henry Willard was born in Westminster Vermont in 1822. He came to the attention of Benjamin Ogle Tayloe when the latter visited his wife's family near Troy New York in the 1840s. The owner of the City Hotel at 14th Street and Pennsylvania Avenue, Tayloe leased and then sold the property to Henry Willard. Willard's Hotel, as it then was called, was a success from the start due to its proprietor and the prosperity that came to Washington in the 1850s. Starting with President Pierce in 1852, it became common for presidents to lodge there prior to their inauguration. By 1858, the hotel had expanded north to F Street. It was the center for Unionists to congregate whereas the National Hotel at 6th Street was frequented by Southern sympathizers.

One of the great moments of Willard's Hotel was in March 1861 when it was the temporary home of President-elect Lincoln prior to his inauguration. Lincoln walked over from Willard's with Secretary of State William Seward on the morning of his inauguration to worship at St John's Church at nearby Lafayette Park. Out-going President James Buchanan then picked Lincoln up at Willard's; despite threats, they rode down Pennsylvania Avenue in an open carriage to the U.S. Capitol for the inauguration. The term "lobbyist" was coined to describe the crowds seeking jobs and contracts that congregated in the lobby of Willard's to await Lincoln at the time of his inauguration.

The 1860s brought Henry Willard and his hotel fame and fortune during the Civil War and the beginnings of the Gilded Age that brought many more visitors to Washington. Henry Willard and his brothers became very prosperous members of the Washington business community. For example, Henry Willard was associated with Alexander Shepherd on the Board of Public Works during the Territorial form of government in the early 1870s. He was particularly involved in encouraging the tree plantings that characterize Washington henceforth. .

CHAPTER 6
AMERICAN PLACES

There are somewhat more than thirty places whose names are on the streets of Washington. The earlier use of bi-syllable American place names persists mainly in the southeast area. Evenly divided between names of towns and of bodies of water, both the towns and natural bodies of water are almost entirely from the area east of the Mississippi River and mainly the area east of the Alleghenies.

Albemarle. The major estuary of the coast of North Carolina, Albemarle Sound is bound by the coastal islands called the Outer Banks. Kitty Hawk on the Outer Banks is famous for the inaugural flight by the Wright Brothers. It is still an important area for local fisheries and part of the Intercoastal Inland Waterway. The Roanoke River is one of the major rivers emptying into the Sound and the island of the same name in its southwest recalls the first English settlement in the 16th century. This "Lost Colony" founded by Sir Walter Raleigh. was the forerunner of the more lasting one at Jamestown on the Chesapeake Bay founded in 1607.

During the Civil War, Union General Ambrose Burnside made his mark by his successful expedition in early 1862 that occupied the local area preventing its use for Confederate blockade runners. The success of the Confederate ironclad *CSS Virginia* in Hampton Roads in March 1862 led to an extraordinary local effort to build a comparable boat to lift the Union blockade of this area. The ironclad ram called the *CSS Albemarle*, built in a makeshift shipyard up the Roanoke River, entered the Sound in April 1864. It controlled the area, temporarily lifting the blockade until October 1864 when it in turn was destroyed by a "torpedo" on a Union gunboat during a daring raid.

The name also recalls the career of George Monck, the 1st Duke of Albemarle. Born in 1608 in Devon to a noble family, he had a career as a soldier on the continent. He was notable for his bravery at the Siege of Breda in the Netherlands in 1637. Back in England, he served the Royalist cause during the English Civil War and then Cromwell in his conquest of Ireland. He was in control of the remnants of Cromwell's New Model Army in Scotland during the inter regnum following the death of Oliver Cromwell. The support of his army assured the restoration of the Stuart monarchy in 1660. The grateful Charles II showered Monk with wealth and titles including membership among the Lord Proprietors of the new colony named Carolina.

Argonne was the name of the forest in northeast France where American troops participated in the Grand Offensive starting in September 1918 that ended World War I.

Austin. The capital of Texas since 1839, Austin is on the Colorado River in central Texas at the terminus of the Chisholm Trail. It is also the site of the University of Texas. Previously called Waterloo, it was named after the recently died Stephen F. Austin when it became the capital. Born in 1793 in the mining area of southwestern Virginia, Austin's family moved in his childhood to the lead mining area of Missouri. He graduated from Transylvania University in Lexington Kentucky in 1810 before moving to Arkansas and then Louisiana where he studied law. In 1821, he took up his dead father's extensive land grant in Texas and succeeded in bringing settlers to what was then a province of Mexico. These settlers eventually revolted against Santa Anna to gain independence in 1835 at the Battle of San Jacinto under Sam Houston. Austin was Secretary of State of the Republic of Texas for the short time before his death.

Bataan is the name of the mountainous peninsula to the west of Manila Bay where American and Filipino troops took their stand after the Japanese capture of Manila in January 1942. The defense lines were successively outflanked until the army command was forced to retreat to the island of Corregidor in April 1942. Those American and Filipino soldiers captured were required to march to their prison camp in an infamous "Death March."

Bangor is the main commercial center of eastern and northern Maine. Thirty miles up the Penobscot River from Penobscot Bay, it is the county seat of the county with the same name. A major lumber port in the 19th century, the surrounding forests is now devoted to making paper. An active center for the anti-slavery movement, the surrounding area sent many soldiers to fight for the Union including the famous 20th Maine Regiment that held Little Round Top at Gettysburg under Joshua Chamberlain. .

Brandywine River (Creek). Rising in Chester County in southeastern Pennsylvania, the two branches unite to form the Brandywine Creek to join the Christina River just past Wilmington. This last river then joins the Delaware River in its way to the Delaware Bay. The area was settled by the Lenape (Delaware) Algonquin speaking tribe. There was an early settlement of Swedes and Dutch at Fort Christina at the confluence of the rivers (the site of present-day Wilmington) with the name of the river derives probably from the Dutch name for the drink. Under English control, it became part of William Penn's Charter in 1682 when he made his famous treaty with the local Amerindians.

During the Revolutionary War, it was the site of a battle in September 1777. British General William Howe landed troops at the head of Chesapeake Bay on his way to Philadelphia. Washington tried to block his advance at Chadds Ford but was outflanked by a crossing to the north. Howe went on to occupy Philadelphia forcing the Continental Congress to move temporarily to York Pennsylvania.

The local settlers took advantage of the 160 foot drop of the river near Chadds Ford to build mills for grain and paper. The local "Brandywine Superfine Flour" became famous. Chadds Ford also became the site in 1803 for the Eleutherian Mills, making gunpowder for the Eleuthere Irenee du Pont de Nemours Company.

Camden is on the New Jersey shore of the Delaware River opposite Philadelphia. It thrived as the terminus of the Camden and Amboy Railroad that was from 1834 an important link, with ferries at either end, on the route between Philadelphia and New York. Formerly, the home of the Victor Talking Machine Company (RCA Victor), the New York Shipbuilding Company and Campbell's Soup, the city has been steadily losing population with the departure of its manufacturing base.

Champlain. The founder in 1608 of the colony of New France and the town of Quebec, Samuel Champlain also gave his name to the lake that forms part of the boundary between the states of New York and Vermont. It was the site of a combined naval and army American operation in 1814 during the War of 1812 that caused the withdrawal of an invading force. That victory brought recognition to Alexander Macomb as the commander of the land forces at Plattsburgh New York.

Chesapeake Bay. Rivers from the Susquehanna south to the York and James including the Potomac, the Patuxent and the Patapsco form the largest estuary in the United States. The Chesapeake Bay is actually the Valley of the Susquehanna River drowned by the rise in sea level after the end of the Ice Age. The name is a corruption of the local Algonquin speakers' word for "Great Water."

The earliest European settlers entered the Bay in 1607 at Cape Henry, named after the eldest son of James I, to settle at Jamestown on the James River. Captain John Smith explored the area from 1607 to 1609 and published his map in 1612. The tidewater area of early settlement in both Maryland and Virginia was the home during the next one hundred and fifty years of an aristocratic planter culture based on the cultivation of tobacco increasingly by African slaves.

During the Revolutionary War, the Battle of the Chesapeake (of the Capes) in September 1781 was a crucial strategic French naval victory. The attempt of the British fleet to reinforce or evacuate Cornwallis under siege at Yorktown was prevented by the French under Comte de Grasse. It led to the surrender of the army of General Cornwallis at Yorktown in October 1781, the last battle of the Revolutionary War.

During the War of 1812, the British fleet under Admiral Cockburn invaded the Bay, entered the Patuxent River to march overland to capture Washington in August 1814 and burn the public buildings. The British fleet then reached as far as Fort McHenry on the Patapsco at Baltimore in September 1814 before turning back. The observation of the flag still flying after the night of bombardment inspired Francis Scott Key to compose the poem that forms the basis of the national anthem.

During the Civil War, the Union blockade was strangling the export of Confederate cotton and the import of needed war materiel. The overwhelming Union naval superiority required innovative strategies. One was to equip the *USS Merrimack*, captured at the Norfolk Navy Yard, with a ram and ironclad sides. On March 8th 1862, the rechristened *CSS Virginia* was able to destroy several wooden-hulled Union ships and looked eventually to overcome the superior union naval force enforcing the blockade. During the following night, the *USS Monitor* arrived from New York where it had been designed and built under the direction of the Swedish-American inventor John Ericsson. The Monitor was also innovative in that it contained stern guns in a steam driven turret providing a wide excursion of fire as well as being clad in iron plate for protection. The first battle in history between ironclads occurred the next day with the withdrawal of the Confederate ship.

Chicago arose at the southwest corner of Lake Michigan where there was a short portage; and then with the development of the Illinois and Michigan Canal in the 1830s a direct connection for shipping from the Great Lakes to the Illinois River and thence to the Mississippi. The arrival of the railroad at the same time made it the center for transportation. Now it is also the air hub with O'Hare Airport the world's second busiest. The center for manufacturing, meatpacking and retail for the entire Mid-West for much of its history, it is still the 3rd largest city in the United States.

Columbia(n). This important east-west road was actually named after the "Columbian College in the District of Columbia" that had first been situated on the adjacent "College Hill."

George Washington had, on many occasions, declared his interest in a university in the Federal City. He mentioned it in his first Message to Congress in January 1790; again in the Message of December 1796; and planned to insert it in his Farewell Address. He had in mind an institution that would develop friendships among future leaders; and thus help to reduce sectionalism and where youth could experience the sessions of Congress and the courts; to hear public men, and experience the development of public policy. Moreover, he devoted several pages to this purpose in his last Will and made for it his largest bequest of 5,000 pounds in his shares of the Potomack Company Canal. Other proposals made by Thomas Jefferson and James Madison were also not acted upon. The Jesuit Georgetown College arose on the heights above Georgetown in 1789.

However, the plan for a national university was acted upon independently by Luther Rice while a Baptist missionary in the national capital. Founded in 1821, the "Columbian College in the District of Columbia" bought land in the Mount Pleasant area of Meridian Hill, north of Boundary Road, During the Civil War, and military encampments took over portions of the College Hill campus. They built the 800-bed Columbian College Hospital, the 1300-bed Carver Hospital and, close by, the 1600-bed Mount Pleasant Hospital.

The name was changed to "Columbian University" in 1873 in light of additional Schools of Pharmacy, School of Fine Arts and the Corcoran School of Science, the last secured by the gift of land given by Corcoran called "Trinidad." In 1882, the university moved its facilities from College Hill to the area of H Street between 13th and 15th Streets in recognition of the school becoming a "night school" for students and also using part-time faculty.

Funds were a recurrent problem; the lack of support from the Baptist Convention led to separation of the College from the denomination. In 1904, in recognition of a gift from the never completed "George Washington Memorial," the name of the university was changed to the "George Washington University." Following the reorganization of the University in 1908 toward a greater degree of professional faculty, it had become almost entirely a "day school" and looked once more to the provision of dormitories for student life. In 1912, the first of the buildings at 20th and G Streets in Foggy Bottom was bought with funds provided by Abram Lisner. The former home of the Saint Rose's Industrial School, it became the first GW dormitory, known as Old Lisner Hall. The childless owner of the Palais Royal department store, Lisner became a major benefactor in the early 20th century with the building of the Lisner Library and the Lisner Auditorium.

Cloyd Heck Marvin was the university's president from 1927 to 1959. During his long tenure, the university increased its presence in the Foggy Bottom area with the tripling of the size of faculty and the doubling of the student body. Marvin was particularly interested in the development of the Department of Physics that included Edward Teller as one of its faculty;

Marvin sponsored a series of international conferences on theoretical physics in the 1930s that brought such luminaries as Niels Bohr to the campus. Marvin was criticized for reducing the influence of the liberal arts in the curriculum and producing graduates to perform primarily as government functionaries—"men in grey flannel suits."

The opening of Lisner Auditorium in the 1940s provided the best-equipped theater in the city and, prior to the Kennedy Center, the center for most music and dramatic performances. At its opening performance of *St Joan*, Ingrid Bergman protested against its policy of segregation to world-wide notice. Under Marvin, GW was still a relatively small Southern university, with a tacitly segregated student body mainly living in the suburbs Marvin insisted, despite student protests, on maintaining segregation in the Auditorium and then of the University. The building of a student center in the 1970s became another focus of student protests. Despite student interest in naming it in memory of the killed Kent State students, it was named in honor of the former president based on a donation by his widow.

Under subsequent presidents, the George Washington University has grown in its enrollment, its diversity and its reputation as a leading urban university in the spirit of the vision of George Washington as a national university in the nation's capital.

Corregidor is the name of the island fortified to protect against a naval attack on Manila Bay in the Philippines. Manila was captured by the Japanese by land after an invasion on the north of the island of Luzon in December 1941 soon after the attack on Pearl Harbor that incapacitated the American Pacific Fleet. After the capture of Bataan, from which it received its water and ammunition, the island fortress could not hold out and was captured by the Japanese in May 1942.

Cumberland River. Rising in Harlan County in southeastern Kentucky, the Cumberland River flows west past the 70 foot drop of Cumberland Falls through Tennessee past Nashville to empty into the Ohio River at Smithland Kentucky near its confluence with the Mississippi River. The important Cumberland Water Gap through the Appalachian Mountains and the river were both named in 1750 after Prince William, Duke of Cumberland. The younger son of George II, he was also the commander of the British Army and famous for his victory in 1746 over the Jacobite Stuart Pretender at Culloden in Scotland.

An important route for western settlement, the Cumberland River also became a major commercial route for cotton and other commodities before the Civil War. Nashville became an important river port. In January 1862, the first Union victory of the entre war occurred at Mill Springs along the eastern Cumberland under the command of Brigadier General George Thomas. The February 1862 Union capture of Fort Henry (at the mouth of the Tennessee River) and neighboring Fort Donelson (on the Cumberland River) under Brigadier General Ulysses Grant and the naval commander Andrew Hull Foote broke the major Confederate defensive line and led to the occupation of Nashville. Union control of the Cumberland River during the rest of the war, albeit contested by guerilla warfare, was crucial for supplying the army fighting in Tennessee.

After the Civil War, the cultivation of cotton was replaced by more varied agriculture that still used the steamboat in the more mountainous upper reaches of the river to carry lumber and other commodities. The coal of the non-navigable even higher reaches of the river between the Gap and the Cumberland Falls was tapped in the 20th century by the railroad that made Harlan Kentucky synonymous with coal. Following the 1930s, along with the Tennessee River, the Cumberland has been harnessed by the dams built by the U.S. Corps of Engineers to provide electricity and flood control.

Davenport. A city in eastern Iowa on the Mississippi River, it is the county seat of Scott County. The county was named after General Winfield Scott, commander during the recently ended war pushing "Black Hawk" back from entering the territory of Illinois. Chief Keokuk of the Sauk tribe gave land to Marguerite, the granddaughter of a Sac Chief and the wife of Antoine LeClaire. The latter founded on that land in 1836 the town named after his friend Colonel George Davenport stationed at nearby Fort Armstrong.

Halfway between Chicago and Des Moines, Davenport flourished particularly after the Rock Island Railroad built a bridge crossing the Mississippi River from Rock Island Illinois to Davenport. The first bridge across the Mississippi, it was built in two parts via the Rock Island in the middle of the river. Abraham Lincoln served as a lawyer in the late 1850s defending the railroad when it was sued for damages incurred by a ship using the river. He won the case by establishing the principle that rights existed equally for traffic crossing the river as well as those steamships going north south on the river..

Erie. One of the Great Lakes that divides Ohio from Ontario (then Upper Canada), it figured prominently in the naval battles during the War of 1812. Starting in the spring of 1813, Oliver H. Perry created an American fleet that in September 1813 was victorious over the British in a hard won battle. "We have met the enemy and he is ours" was his iconic statement. The Battle of Lake Erie changed the balance of power on the Great Lakes and cemented U.S. control of the Northwest Territory.

Frankford was settled by Germans under the auspices of the Frankfurt Company in 1684 immediately northeast of the original city of Philadelphia. Alongside Frankford Creek on the Delaware River, it was an early manufacturing center with gristmill and textile mills. The borough was annexed to the Center City in 1854 and connected to it by rapid transit.

Galveston is on the island off the coast whose natural port was the first in Texas. Founded in 1825 after Mexican independence, it served for a short time as the capital of the Republic of Texas. The Galveston Plan was an effort sponsored by the "Industrial Recovery Office" of the Jewish Colonization Society in the 1890s to land Jewish immigrants at a port other than New York. This would enable them to settle in towns in the Mississippi River Valley rather than in the Lower East Side.

A thriving port for the export of cotton, Galveston competed with New Orleans until the hurricane of September 6th 1900 inundated the island. It has never recovered and its port has been superseded by the artificial Houston Ship Channel.

Hartford. The capital of Connecticut, it is on the Connecticut River at the site of its confluence with the Park River. Named after Hertford, the English home of one of its early settlers; it was founded in 1639 by a group from Cambridge Massachusetts led by Thomas Hooker. His sermon "Fundamental Order" claimed that government be based on the consent of the governed, a notion incorporated into the Connecticut Constitution and then the U.S. Constitution, hence Connecticut is known as "The Constitution State."

A center for abolition of slavery, its inhabitants in the mid-19th century included Harriet Beecher Stowe, author of *Uncle Tom's Cabin*. Highly prosperous during the early industrialization of the Connecticut River Valley, it became the seat of the Wadsworth Atheneum, a center for book publishing, as well as for the insurance industry.

Harvard College. The college in Cambridge Massachusetts was founded in 1636, the first in the English colonies. It was named after John Harvard, A graduate of Cambridge University in Cambridge England; he was an early benefactor who left his library and a substantial bequest to the struggling new school. Closely connected with the local Boston Puritan clergy of the Congregational Church for most of its early history, it became secularized in the early 19th century. After the Civil War, under President Charles Eliot, it became a major university in the German model. In the 20th century, particularly under President James Conant it became more diverse in its student body and curriculum while gathering the largest endowment of any private American university.

Joliet is a town southwest of Chicago on the Des Plaines River. Founded in the 1830s after the success of the war expelling Black Hawk, it was named after the Frenchman Louis Jolliet who paddled on its river with Father Jacques Marquette in 1673.

Kanawha River. Rising in the southeast and flowing northwestward past Charleston and St Albans, the Kanawha River lies entirely within the state of West Virginia and empties into the Ohio River at Point Pleasant. In the 17th century, the Seneca tribe of the Iroquois Confederacy drove out the local Conoy tribe from which the river receives its name. An uninhabited hunting ground for the Iroquois on the east, the Shawnees on the north and the Lenape (Delaware) on the south, its first European settlement was Lewisburg in the latter part of the 18th century.

The lower river was not navigable until the 1840s; the upper river not until following the 1870s. The valley is the major industrial center of the state based upon its resources of coal and natural gas.

Kenyon College. The oldest private college in Ohio, it was founded in 1824 by the Episcopal Bishop Philander Chase. The British Lord Kenyon was one of the earliest benefactors. Its Gothic Revival campus has some of the earliest buildings of that style in the United States. Its English Department is particularly noteworthy for its sponsorship of the *Kenyon Review*.

Newark. Although there are several towns that carry that name in the United States, Newark in New Jersey is most prominent. Founded in the 17th century by persons from Milford, Connecticut seeking a more strictly religious environment, the name New-Ark reflects its religious origin. As early as 1680, leather tanning became its leading industry. The bark from the local tamarack tree provided the tannin necessary for the tanning process. By 1837, there were also 155 patent leather manufacturers. The first plastic, called "Celluloid" was invented there.

In 1840, the Ballantine Brewery was founded that grew together with a large German population following the Revolution of 1848. Other businesses in the 19th century were the Mutual Benefit Life Insurance Company in 1845 and the Prudential Insurance Company in 1875. Industrialization reached its zenith in the era ending in 1930 when its population approached a half-million and whose vibrant Jewish immigrant culture and their descendants is documented by its native son Philip Roth.

Northampton. Decimated by smallpox brought by the early Europeans, the early Algonquin speaking inhabitants were driven out in the early 17th century by Mohawks of the Iroquois Confederation. Settled by Europeans in the 1630s from Springfield Massachusetts, it was named for the English town of origin of one of its early settlers. A city in the Connecticut River Valley, it is the county seat of Hampshire County Massachusetts. The home of the Clarke School for the Deaf (1867) and Smith College for Women (1871), it is the northern outpost of the Connecticut River Valley "Knowledge Corridor."

Oneida. The name of the town in central New York reflects the local Amerindian nation that was part of the five-nation Iroquois Confederacy. Unlike the other nations that supported the British during the Revolutionary War, the majority of the Oneida supported the American colonists. They therefore remained in the United States rather than migrate to Canada after American independence. First assigned what amounted to a large reservation, their lands were gradually reduced to appease the land hungry veterans. They were forced to relocate to Wisconsin with some migrating to Upper Canada (Ontario).

Ontario. Separated from "Lower Canada" by the Constitutional At of 1791, "Upper Canada," defined by its site on the St Lawrence River, received its own legislature. Protestant in religion and English-speaking, it had been settled by many of the British Empire Loyalists exiled from the newly formed United States; and later by migrants from New York State in the process of going west. At one time, it was more "American," than the British of its overlords. Called "West Canada" in 1840, it entered as "Ontario" into the Confederation of Canada in 1867. The Canadian federal capital of Ottawa sits on the border of the two first major provinces of Quebec and Ontario.

Portland is the largest city in Maine. Founded in the 17th century on Casco Bay, it was the capital for a time when Maine first became a state in 1820. Named after the place on the coast of Dorset, it flourished in the 19th century when it served as an ice free port for Canadian exports until the nationalized Canadian railroad diverted traffic to Halifax.

Potomac River. The North Branch rises in West Virginia to join the South Branch at Hampshire County West Virginia then to join the Shenandoah at Harper's Ferry. The Potomac River forms the boundary between the states of Maryland and Virginia, then Virginia and the District of Columbia on its way to the Chesapeake Bay. The name derives from the Algonquin word for "trading place." The river falls from the Piedmont to the coastal plain near the boundary of the District of Columbia at Little Falls after entering the rocky gorge of Great Falls. The port of Georgetown was founded in the 1750s at the river's head of navigation at the mouth of Rock Creek.

George Washington spent his early life surveying its watershed for land speculators. He saw its importance for connecting the eastern seaboard of the newly independent country to the Ohio Valley. This was a factor for the selection of the site of the federal Seat of Government on the coastal plain at the confluence of the Potomac and its Eastern Branch (the Anacostia) To aid its commercial development, George Washington helped found the "Patowmack Company" to build locks to bypass obstructions such as the rapids at Great Falls. With this earlier effort unsuccessful due to variation in the river flow, the Chesapeake & Ohio (C&O) Canal was started in the 1830s to run alongside the river, reaching Cumberland Maryland but not its goal of the Ohio River. The concomitant building of the Baltimore & Ohio (B&O) Railroad superseded the C&O Canal by reaching Wheeling on the Ohio River making Baltimore rather than Washington DC the port of choice for the produce of the Ohio Valley.

During the Civil War, the river was the boundary between the Confederacy and the Union. The protection of the Federal capital bordering the Potomac was one of the important priorities during the entire war. Immediately after the secession of Virginia, Union troops occupied Alexandria and Arlington Heights. After the debacle of the 1st Battle of Bull Run, a ring of defensive forts was built in 1861-1862 around Washington to protect against attack from across the Potomac River during its low water months. General Lee and his Army of Northern Virginia did cross in September 1862 to be driven back at Antietam; then in July 1863 to be driven back at Gettysburg. General Jubal Early crossed again in July 1864 to be driven back only at the outskirts of the city by the defensive line at Fort Stevens.

First traversed by a bridge at Little Falls in 1798, the first bridge connecting the Virginia shore directly to the City of Washington was the Long Bridge at 14th Street. When first built in 1809, the wide expanse of the Potomac River had two separate channels with a sea of mudflats between them. The original bridge thus had draw spans, and sections with partial causeways and piles of rock to hold it all down during periodic ice floes. The original northern channel adjacent to the Washington shore was relatively narrow; there was frequent back-up of water out of Tiber Creek with flooding onto Pennsylvania Avenue by the frozen river.

Princeton. The town is the site of the college founded as the College of New Jersey in 1746 that moved to Princeton in 1756. It was the fourth institution of higher education in the colonies after Harvard, The College of William & Mary and Yale. Its first building called Nassau Hall was named after the House of William III, the king who came to England after the Glorious Revolution of 1688 deposing the Catholic James II. Founded by "New Light" Presbyterians to train ministers, it evolved under John Witherspoon, its president from 1768 to 1794, to become a broader institution graduating men like James Madison.

During the Revolutionary War, the American victory at Princeton in January 1777 immediately after the successful raid at Christmas on Trenton lifted American spirits. Also for a period in 1783, the Continental Congress met in Nassau Hall at the college when it left Philadelphia because of lack of protection from Revolutionary War soldiers seeking payment.

After the Civil War, President James McCosh rebuilt the school; Woodrow Wilson as president starting in 1902 increased its academic standing. The founding in 1939 of the Institute for Advanced Study enhanced the university's status further when Albert Einstein became its most famous resident scholar.

Providence is both the capital and the largest city in Rhode Island on the Providence River at the head of Narragansett Bay. It was founded in 1636 by Roger Williams who was a religious outcast from the Massachusetts Bay Colony. He gave its name in recognition of the "haven God's merciful providence had provided." An early center of textile manufacture, it remained until recently an industrial center for jewelry and silver.

Quebec. The city on the St Lawrence River was founded in 1608 by Samuel de Champlain to be the first in New France, The name derives from the Algonquin for "where the river narrows" appropriate for its site on the bluffs of the narrowed river. In the early 17th century, Cardinal Richelieu settled its first French peasant farmers from Normandy and Brittany. The absolutist Louis XIV later established direct royal control with appointment of an Intendant and Governor to share power with the bishop. The three pillars of the community were the autocratic royal government, the adoption of the feudal system of land tenure under the rule of the seignior and the Catholic Church. The prototype early ecclesiastical leader Bishop Laval arrived in 1659 and died in Quebec in 1708. The Church was committed to the establishment of a French Catholic colony in the New World where both the religious and national elements were inextricably intertwined. French Canada was unique in the integration of the Church in the daily life of its inhabitants.

The British victory on the Plains of Abraham outside the town in 1759 led to the cession of New France to Britain in 1763 at the end of the Seven Years War. The Royal Proclamation establishing "Canada" limited its territory to that along the St Lawrence River. However, the "Quebec Act" of 1774 essentially re-established the boundary of what had been New France extending Quebec to include the Great Lakes to the Ohio River Valley. By also impinging on the ability of the English colonists to settle west of the seacoast colonies, the Quebec Act was one of the grievances leading to the American Revolution. In the 1783 treaty ending that war,

Britain ceded most of that territory (The Northwest Territory) to the newly formed United States.

The Constitutional Act of 1791 established the Province of Canada with Quebec now called "Lower Canada," then in 1840 "East Canada," then as the Province of Quebec, united with the other early provinces to form Canada in the "Confederation Act" of 1867.

Raleigh is the capital of North Carolina and its second largest city. The county seat of Wake County, it was first settled in the 1770s and became the state capital in the 1780s since it was more defensible than coastal New Bern. One of the few towns in the United States specifically designed to be a capital city, the Capitol building is in the middle of the central public square with streets extending in all four directions.

Saint Louis was first settled in the 1760s by French Canadians but developed as the major port on the Mississippi River only after the Louisiana Purchase of 1803. Central to the struggle to retain the slave holding border state of Missouri in the Union, St Louis, with its large population of pro-Union German immigrants, was the scene of turmoil in the spring of 1861. The 4th largest city in the United States post-Civil War, there was talk in the 1870s of moving the national capital from Washington to this more central location. It is the site of the important Eads Bridge crossing the Mississippi River.

Savannah. The original settlement in Georgia in 1733, it was founded by James Oglethorpe as a refuge for debtors. On the Savannah River, the derivation of its name is unclear. During the Revolutionary War, the city was captured by the British in 1778. The following year, an army under General Benjamin Lincoln supported by French naval forces under Admiral d'Estaing besieged the city in a failed attempt to recapture it. One of the bloodiest battles of the war, the Polish cavalry officer Casmir Pulaski was killed in the attempt and Peter L'Enfant was wounded and captured.

An important port, it was blockaded by the Union capture of Fort Pulaski at the mouth of the Savannah River in April 1862. The siege that preceded its capture was notable for the success of rifled cannon in sending projectiles accurately from a far distance. The city itself was captured on 25th December 1864 by General Sherman approaching from land on his March through Georgia.

Tewksbury. Named after the English town, it was settled along the Shawsheen River in north central Massachusetts (named after the local Shawshin tribe).

Trenton. The capital of New Jersey, it is in the center of that state. Founded in 1679 by Quakers from Handsworth (Sheffield) England at the falls of the Delaware River, it received its present name in 1720s from the name of Robert Trent, its new owner.

It is most famous for the raid conducted by Washington's Continental Army on the Hessians on 26th December 1776. After the famous iconic crossing of the icy Delaware River, the surprise attack was the first American victory of the war.

Williamsburg. The settlers at original English settlement founded on marshy ground along the James River were subject to illness because of the local mosquitoes. After an Indian uprising, a palisade was established further up the peninsula in 1638 to guard against attack. Called "Middle Plantation," the College of William & Mary was established there on its higher ground in 1693, the second school of higher education in the colonies. After the statehouse in Jamestown burned down, the capital was moved to what was now called Williamsburg, after William III the recently installed Dutch Protestant king.

The Capitol building faced the college building designed by Sir Christopher Wren connected by the Duke of Gloucester Street. The Virginia House of Burgesses meeting in the Capitol was the first representative assembly in the colonies. Founded in 1619, it followed the action of the London Company in permitting settlers to own land and elect representatives. The House issued in 1769 the "Virginia Resolutions" protesting the British occupation of Boston and the imposition of taxes by the British Parliament. After the Declaration of Independence, the House became the Virginia General Assembly, the legislative branch of the Commonwealth of Virginia. In 1780, the capital moved farther up the James River to Richmond to protect against invasion by the British.

The city of Williamsburg faded, sustained only by the Eastern State Hospital for the Insane founded in the 1770s and the College of William & Mary. In the spring of 1862 during the Civil War, it was the site of a siege for a time by the forces of General George McClellan. In the 1930s, Colonial Williamsburg was restored as a project of the Rockefeller family.

Wilmington. The largest city in Delaware, it was founded in 1638 by Swedes as Fort Christina at the confluence of the Christina river and Brandywine Creek. Its name reflected the Swedish 17th century queen. Part of the area under the control of the Penn family, the name was changed to Wilmington in 1739 to honor the Earl of Wilmington. Born Spencer Compton, the third son of the Earl of Northampton, he was active from 1696 as a Whig member of the House of Commons before being raised to the peerage.

Xenia. A town in southwestern Ohio near Dayton, it was founded in 1803 at the forks of the Shawnee Creeks. The county seat of Greene County (named after General Nathanael Greene); the unusual name of the town is the Greek word for hospitality. It flourished for a time during the coming of the Little Miami Railroad after 1843.

Yuma. In the extreme southwestern corner of Arizona, it is at the site of Fort Yuma near the confluence of the Gila and Colorado Rivers where the river is at its narrowest. The Gateway to California, a steamboat stop starting in the 1850s, the ferry was replaced in 1870 by a railroad bridge.

SECTION III
WASHINGTON'S OUTDOOR PUBLIC SCULPTURE

INTRODUCTION

The most important sculpture in the history of the city of Washington was one that was never erected. Peter L'Enfant had outlined in his original plan two means to unite the major public buildings. There was an urban relationship along Pennsylvania Avenue with "reciprocity of view" between the Congress House and the President's Palace. This was to be complemented by a landscape that extended from the Congress House west to a Monument dedicated to George Washington and from there north to the President's Palace.

An equestrian statue in the model of the grand monarchical prototype was proposed in a unanimous resolution passed by the Continental Congress in 1783. At a time when Congress itself was at low ebb in exile in Princeton New Jersey, it sought legitimacy by association with the victorious general. Congress recommended that the statue be bronze with the Hero represented in Roman dress holding a truncheon in his right hand and his head encircled by a laurel wreath. This design was analogous to the statue of Louis XV .in Gabriel's Place Louis XV, also following the original imperial example of Marcus Aurelius reinstalled in Rome in the Campidoglio.

Later, when Congress had voted to build the Seat of Government on the banks of the Potomac, George Washington agreed with Peter L'Enfant that the statue would be on the Mall at the intersection of the lines west and south from the future Capitol and President's House. The 1783 Resolution and the opportunity to create an equestrian statue of George Washington helped induce Jean-Baptiste Houdon, the greatest sculptor of his day, to come to this country in 1785 to make sketches of George Washington at Mount Vernon. This statue was never erected. The cost was one consideration for the anti-Federalists; another problem remained of how to represent authority in a republic opposed to its traditional monarchical form. Washington had been recognized for his authority based on his readiness to give up his military command; later by his abdication after two terms as president.

In the tradition of the original planned statue of George Washington, the streets of his city came to recall mainly military heroes. They fulfill Peter L'Enfant's hope for his plan's numerous green spaces to embody great Americans. The chronological organization of this section reflects the list of the wars that provide the context in which their heroes were commemorated as the United States emerged as a nation tempered by war.

The selection of statues to be illustrated is determined by those that are exemplary for aesthetic or political reasons.

CHAPTER 7
STATUES OF PRE-CIVIL WAR FIGURES

There were only two statues installed on Washington's streets prior to the Civil War. The technology for casting equestrian statues was not available in the United States until solved in the 1850s. They celebrate victors in the Revolutionary War and the War of 1812. In the 1870s, along with those of Civil War generals, further equestrian statues celebrate victors of earlier wars including the Mexican War. After 1900, with the United States looking to its status in the world, once again there was a recrudescence of interest in those who had aided the colonists during the Revolutionary War.

7.1 The Revolutionary War

George Washington and the Washington Monument on the Mall (1845/1884)

The plan of Peter L'Enfant to establish a monument honoring the father of the country as the centerpiece of the Mall was eventually fulfilled but not in the form first envisaged.

In 1833, after the centennial of the birth of George Washington, the long-time Federalist Chief Justice John Marshall was the first president of the Washington National Monument Society. Its goal was to install a Monument at that site on the Mall indicated by L'Enfant. During the next 50 years before its completion, the progress of the Monument varied in accordance with the fortunes of the country. The first drive, launched in 1833, had raised $36,000 by 1836. An architectural competition was won by Robert Mills in 1845.

Born in South Carolina in 1781 to a Scottish father, Mills was the first American trained as an architect from the outset. He was singled out by his father to receive a classical education at Charleston College. He then apprenticed to James Hoban, accompanying him to Washington to work on the Presidential Mansion. He then worked under Thomas Jefferson at Monticello and then under Benjamin Henry Latrobe, America's first professional architect. Mills had been responsible for building a number of fireproof custom house structures that brought him to the attention of Andrew Jackson looking for a replacement for the government buildings recently destroyed by fire. Appointed Supervising Architect of the U.S. Treasury, Mills was responsible in the early 1830s for building the Ionic colonnaded west wing of the U.S. Treasury alongside the White House and the south wing of the U.S. Patent Office with Doric-columned portico.

The winning plan by Mills for the "Washington National Monument" was a grand circular Doric-colonnaded building 100 feet high to serve as a National Pantheon of Revolutionary War heroes surmounted by George Washington driving a four-horse chariot characteristic of a Roman triumph. From this replica of the Pantheon would spring a 500 foot obelisk shaft unadorned aside from a simple star placed within 50 feet of the summit. From the start, the obelisk was designed to be the tallest building in the world. With $87,000 in hand, the cornerstone was laid on July 4, 1848 on land donated near the site originally destined for the equestrian statue. The speaker at the cornerstone laying was Robert Winthrop, an old student of Daniel Webster, a Whig and Speaker of the House. His theme was a recurrent one: the value of Washington as a symbol of unity at a time when centrifugal tendencies were becoming more prominent.

The obelisk rose to 150 feet in 1854 before construction stopped. Stones had been contributed by the various states and from foreign countries. For example, Greece contributed a stone from the Parthenon. The stone contributed by Pope Pius IX from the Roman Temple of Concordia apparently raised the ire of the American (Know Nothing) Party opposed to Catholic immigration. The opposition of the "Know Nothings" and the other political struggles of the 1850s, as well as the Panic of 1857 brought construction to a stop. During the Civil War, the incomplete stump remained, surrounded by cattle pens and slaughter houses for the benefit of the Union forces. In 1867, Mark Twain described it as "a factory chimney with the top broken off…cow sheds about its base…contented sheep nibbling pebbles in the desert solitudes… tired pigs dozing in the holy calm of its protecting shadow." Its incomplete nature seemed illustrative of the incomplete nature of the capital city and of the scheme of the American union.

The shame of the uncompleted shaft in one speaker's words was "like a maimed finger lifted up in reproach." The Centennial of Independence in 1876 renewed interest in the completion of the monument, but now to be entrusted to the U.S. Army Corps of Engineers. The issue of what Washington represented that had held up his commemoration thus far was laid to rest. It was to be merely an aesthetic decision, to be tasteful but also to be modern; one would be able to rise to the top by an elevator. In accordance with the dimensions of ancient obelisks, the height was fixed at 555 feet as 10 times that of a base of 55 feet. Construction of the obelisk was completed in 1884 with a capstone covered with a shiny tip of the then newly-invented aluminum. Deletion of the temple base designed by Mills changes the meaning of the Monument by no longer placing George Washington within his national historical context. The name "Washington

Monument" captures the change from its original designation as the Washington National Monument.

On its completion, the Monument was the world's tallest structure. Soon superseded by the Eiffel Tower in 1889, it still remains the world's tallest masonry structure. The goal of Mills and the National Monument Society has been fulfilled. It had been "to surpass every other [monument] in the world in elevations and grandeur of proportions …like Washington himself who stands alone in the annals of the world without a model and without a shadow." The final dedication in 1885 once again involved the orator at its first dedication in 1848. In the spirit of the Sun-God of the obelisk's ancient Egyptian origins, Robert Winthrop evoked the sun: "May the earliest day of the rising sun…draw forth from it daily…a strain of national harmony…to strike a responsive chord in every heart throughout the republic." The tallest obelisk in history had become a monument to American technology, to ingenuity and of modern American destiny.

George Washington in Washington Circle (1860)

George Washington is shown in the center of Washington Circle rallying his troops against the British in January 1777 during the Battle of Princeton. This was after the victorious attack on the Hessian troops on Christmas Day 1776 at Trenton. These victories helped hold the Continental Army together at a crucial time.

Figure 10 - Equestrian Statue of George Washington

Congress commissioned this statue, the first equestrian statue of Washington the General in Washington DC, after the statue of Andrew Jackson done by the sculptor Clark Mills had been successfully placed in 1853 in Lafayette Park. Placed in 1860 in this far from central location, it was only the third equestrian statue done in the United States. The head comes from the bust done from life by Houdon at Mount Vernon in 1785 when he came in conjunction with the design of the earlier planned equestrian Washington statue that had never been accomplished.

Nathanael Greene at Stanton Square (1874)

In 1874, Congress funded an equestrian memorial to Major General Nathanael Greene. Originally, from Rhode Island, he was a Revolutionary war hero who successfully engaged in the Southern colonies during 1780 the forces of British General Charles Cornwallis.

The sculptor Henry Kirke Brown was born in 1814 in Massachusetts. After studying painting in Boston, he spent the years 1842 to 1846 in Italy in the study of sculpture. He was renowned for casting his own equestrian statues including that of George Washington in 1856 in Union Square in New York, second only to that of Andrew Jackson in 1853 by Clark Mills in Lafayette Park.

Marquis de Lafayette at southeast corner of Lafayette Park (1891)

It was a full century after the end of the American Revolution before there was recognition of the contribution by several of the important foreign volunteers. Both the name given to the park in which it stands and its site opposite the White House attest to the importance of one of the greatest heroes of the American Revolution. His commitment to its ideals pervaded his entire life. The statue recalls Lafayette seeking help in France in 1778 for the American colonists. He thus contributed to the creation of the alliance with France so crucial to eventual victory.

Standing on the pedestal of the statue are respectively the French naval and army commanders of the forces that were committed to the American cause as a result of the alliance Lafayette helped bring about.

The sculptors Alexandre Falguiere and Marius Mercie were leading exponents of the French School fashionable in America at the end of the 19th century. The former, born in Toulouse in 1831, trained at L'Ecole des Beaux-Arts and won the Prix de Rome in 1859. He also became in 1882 one of the eight sculptors who were members of the highly prestigious Academie des Beaux-Arts, a component in the Institut de France The second and younger sculptor, also born in Toulouse in 1845, was the student of Falguiere and followed him in winning the Prix de Rome in

1868. The Professor of Drawing and Sculpture at the Ecole des Beaux-Arts, he was elected to the Academie Francaise in 1891.

General Jean-Baptiste Comte de Rochambeau at the southwest corner of Lafayette Park (1902)

Although already recognized as one of the figures on the Lafayette pedestal, Congress authorized a statue honoring this military leader so crucial to the final victory at the Battle of Yorktown. A copy of the equestrian statue at his birthplace in Vendome France, its well attended dedication was considered an important international political event. President Theodore Roosevelt was joined by Jules Jusseraud, long time French Ambassador and close presidential friend to emphasize the unity of the world's two great republics.

The first of the 14th Street highway bridges crossing the Potomac, now one-way northbound, was named after Comte de Rochambeau.

General Frederich Wilhelm von Steuben at the northwest corner of Lafayette Park (1910)

Sponsored by Congress, General Frederick Wilhelm von Steuben stands cloaked as he was during the cold winter of 1777-1778 at Valley Forge. A veteran of the army of Frederick the Great in the Seven Years War, he arrived at Valley Forge at the lowest point of the Continental Army. He managed to create a disciplined force that could withstand the British regulars.

Dedicated by President Taft in 1910, a replica was given to the German Kaiser in return for a gift from the latter of a statue of Frederick the Great (placed until 1946 at the Army War College at Fort McNair). As a gesture of goodwill, it was clearly secondary to the precedence already accorded to the French with their two sites directly opposite the White House.

Brigadier-General Thaddeus Kosciuszko at northeast corner of Lafayette Park (1910)

Funded by Americans of Polish extraction, at a time when Poland was still under foreign control, the statue reflects Kosciuszko's dedication to both American and Polish freedom. A military engineer, he volunteered to the Continental Army and helped design fortifications, most notably at Saratoga, which contributed to that important victory. Standing tall atop the pedestal, he is shown on its respective sides aiding an American soldier during the American Revolution and aiding a Polish peasant soldier in the unsuccessful 1794 uprising he led against the Russians.

The sculptor Antoni Popiel was the leading Polish sculptor of his time, working mainly in Cracow and Lvov, both cities of southern Poland then under foreign control. Born in 1866 in Galicia, part of the Austro-Hungarian Empire, he trained in Cracow and Vienna before living in Florence Italy. His design for the statue in Washington was selected by then President Theodore Roosevelt.

Brigadier General Casmir Pulaski at eastern end of Freedom Square (1903/1910)

Figure 11 - General Pulaski

This heroic equestrian statue is of a cavalry leader in the Revolutionary War who died in 1779 at the Battle of Savannah while serving as a volunteer in the Continental Army. A Polish patriot, he wears the uniform of Polish Field Marshal. Like the almost contemporaneous statue of General Kosciuszko, the statue of Pulaski was also at a time when Poland was still under foreign control.

The sculptor Kasimiriez Chodzinski was born in Poland in 1863. He trained at the Art Academy of Cracow and the Vienna Academy of Fine Art. His most important work was in Polish churches. Immigrating to the United States, he settled in Buffalo New York. He was selected by the Pulaski Memorial Commission to represent the high quality of the artists of Polish extraction at a time when the high quality of Polish culture was not well recognized.

General Artemas Ward at Ward Circle (1938)

Long delayed, he was also the last of the military figures to be installed on Massachusetts Avenue. His eponymous circle was late in being laid out as Massachusetts Avenue was extended into Maryland only after 1890. A graduate of Harvard College, a family legacy was given to the university to sponsor what was originally envisaged to be an equestrian statue. Problems with the sculpting of the horse led to the present standing portrait statue.

The sculptor Leonard Crunelle was born in Pays-de-Calais France in 1872. He immigrated to Illinois where he was discovered and mentored by Lorado Taft at the Art Institute of Chicago, a city where his public art is prominent.

Nathan Hale at Justice Department Building (1915/1948)

Standing life size, his feet fettered and about to die, Nathan Hale was the first well-known martyr of the American Revolution. Born in Coventry Connecticut in 1755, he graduated from Yale in 1773. Joining the army after the Battle of Lexington, he served in Boston in 1776. He volunteered to scout the British forces around New York when caught as a spy. About to be executed, his speech contained the words by which he was to be remembered "I only regret that I have but one life to lose for my country."

The statue was commissioned by a Hale biographer and placed at his birthplace in 1915 before being moved to its present site in 1948.

The George Mason Memorial at the 14th Street (George Mason) Bridge (2002)

Figure 12 - The George Mason Memorial

Long delayed and still obscured by the rush of southbound traffic is the surprisingly informal statue of one of the most significant figures in American political history. The Virginia Declaration of Human Rights he authored in 1776 became enshrined in the Virginia State Constitution and later in the Bill of Rights of the U.S. Constitution. It was also the model for the French Declaration of Human Rights of 1789.

On a curved stone bench with his legs crossed, he sits holding a copy of Cicero while on the bench are books by John Locke and J-J Rousseau, the Enlightenment political philosophers. Although rarely used as a pose in the city's numerous monuments, the pose was not uncommon for gentlemen's portraits in the 18th century.

The sculptor Wendy M. Ross trained at the University of Wisconsin and the Rhode Island School of Design. Based on her previous standing statue of George Mason on the campus of his namesake university in Northern Virginia, she was selected by the Trustees of Gunston Hall. She portrayed him sitting with an adjacent cane to recognize his preferences based on the gouty arthritis in his later years.

7.2 The War of 1812

Andrew Jackson in Lafayette Park (1853)

Saturday January 8, 1853 was the anniversary of the Battle of New Orleans in 1815. The first equestrian statue cast in the United States was dedicated in Lafayette Park in honor of Andrew Jackson, the great hero of the War of 1812 and the subsequent two-term president. Attended by a huge crowd including many dignitaries, Senator Stephen A Douglas, the Democratic Party leader, gave the oration in honor of the founder of his party. Douglas spoke of Jackson having been an orphan, finding his family in his country. The speech had been written by Francis P Blair, living nearby in Blair House. He was the former Jacksonian stalwart who had come to Washington from Kentucky in 1832 to work on Jackson's behalf.

Figure 13 - Andrew Jackson Statue

"His statue still stands within sight of the White House with his sword close at hand, ready to ride and ready to fight. His reputation is still as a courageous man, who could not rest, who risked everything…for his one great family—for America." The statue portrays Jackson reviewing his troops on the eve of the Battle of New Orleans and was made with bronze cannon from his capture of Pensacola from the Spanish. The inscription "The Union—it Must be Preserved", although planned by the sculptor, was not actually added until 1909. It echoes Jackson's toast at the famous

Jefferson Day dinner when he drew the line against John Calhoun's toast that placed states rights before the Union.

The sculptor Clark Mills, born 1810 as a poor orphan in Syracuse New York, owned an unusual octagon-shaped foundry in Washington DC, one of the city's few industrial buildings. He broke all precedent in creating the statue of Andrew Jackson. Self-taught, Mills solved a problem that had baffled Leonardo da Vinci by placing Jackson on his charger by weighting the rear legs while the front legs were hollow. Replicas are placed in New Orleans and Nashville.

7.3 The Mexican War

General Winfield Scott in Scott Circle (1874)

By Henry Kirke Brown, also the sculptor of the statue of Revolutionary War General Nathanael Greene, this 1874 equestrian statue honors the hero of the Mexican War. The Scott statue was one of few military memorials paid for by the Congress in its entirety.

The commanding General in the U.S. Army at the start of the Civil War, he retired after 1st Battle of Bull Run in the summer of 1861 and the appointment of George McClellan as head of the Army of the Potomac.

He became Commanding General of the U.S. Army in 1841. His greatest success in the Mexican War was the capture of Mexico City following the route of Cortez after landing at Vera Cruz. After the war, he was the unsuccessful Whig presidential candidate in 1852. Still Commanding General at the outbreak of the Civil War, he remained loyal to the Union, insured the safety of President Lincoln at his inauguration and counseled that the war would be a long one to be won by a blockade and the capture of the Mississippi. Denigrated as merely an "Anaconda" strategy, it proved to be accurate. He earmarked the tribute exacted from the Mexican Government to create the Old Soldiers Home off North Capitol Street. In recognition of his involvement, a statue of Scott also stands there.

CHAPTER 8
THE CIVIL WAR

The 1870s and the generation beyond saw a proliferation of statues memorializing the victors of the Civil War in the city that exemplified the Union during the war. The neo-classical style acquired by training in Italy was superseded by the influence of those trained in Paris at the Ecole des Beaux-Arts tempered by American realism.

The memories of the Civil War still surround Pennsylvania Avenue. One of the most glorious moments of the history of the Avenue was the Grand Review of hundreds of thousands of the men in the Union armies during two days in May 1865. More than the military parade that was first envisaged; not only a tribute to the victorious soldiers, it was an act of rebirth as a reunited nation and a farewell to war. General George Meade, commander of the Army of the Potomac led off the parade of his troops on the first day ending at the White House where he joined General Grant and President Andrew Johnson at the reviewing stand.

Young Marion Hooper from Boston describes "the reviewing platform all covered with the Stars and Stripes...pots of flowers, azaleas, cactus, all in full bloom... almost all the officers in the army had their hands filled with roses, and many had wreaths around their horses' necks...for six hours the old Army of the Potomac marching past...some regiments with nothing but a bare pole, a little bit of rag only hanging a few inches showing where their flag had been...others that had been the Stars and Stripes with one or two stripes hanging, all the rest shot away. It was a strange feeling, to be so intensely happy and triumphant, and yet to feel like crying."

Walt Whitman describes in his diary: "For two days now, the broad spaces of Pennsylvania Avenue along to Treasury hill, and so by detour to the President's house, and up so to Georgetown ...have been alive with a magnificent sight, the returning armies. In their wide ranks stretching clear across the Avenue, I watch them march or ride along...through two whole days –infantry, cavalry, artillery—some 200,000 men."

Washington came to have more equestrian statues than any other city on the continent. A reflection of Washington's significance as the Union capital, Richmond's Monument Avenue is the Confederate counterpart with J.E.B. Stuart, Robert E Lee and Stonewall Jackson. Many of the statues of Civil War generals were sponsored by veterans' organizations. The pedestals and the land were usually donated by the Federal Government. Their dedication at a time of a veterans' encampment included a military parade and an address by high dignitaries usually involving the president. The statues are listed in the order in which they were commissioned or erected. In the 21st century, the meaning of the Civil War has come to include the narrative of slavery and its consequences as well as the purely military.

Freedom atop the U.S. Capitol (1865)

Montgomery Meigs of the U.S. Corps of Engineers was responsible for the ornamentation of the new U.S. Capitol Extension being built in the 1850s. He enlisted Thomas Crawford to sculpt the pediment of the Senate wing. Crawford also completed the allegorical statue of what is commonly called the statue of Freedom, the most prominent feature of the Washington skyline second only to the Washington monument.

Several metamorphoses were necessary before the present statue, more properly called Freedom Triumphant in War and Peace with a sword in hand and shield in the left, became acceptable to Secretary of War Jefferson Davis, Meigs's superior. A slaveholder, Davis particularly objected to the figure's Phrygian cap, symbolic of manumission of Roman slaves. He stated "Its history renders it inappropriate to a people born free and would not be enslaved." A helmet with an eagle's head and feathers suggestive of an Indian headdress was substituted obscuring any suggestion of the extremely sensitive issue of slavery.

Although the plaster cast was completed by 1857 and was later cast in bronze at the Washington foundry of Clark Mills, the statue was finally placed only after the completion of the dome in 1863. The year of the Emancipation Proclamation and Gettysburg, its meaning then became seen as celebrating at the summit of the Capitol the maintenance of the Union under Northern hegemony. Philip Reid, one of those responsible for its casting at the Clark Mills foundry, could celebrate his own freedom after emancipation had occurred in the District of Columbia in April 1862.

The sculptor Thomas Crawford was a member of the first generation of Americans trained in Italy that also included Horatio Greenough and Hiram Powers. Born in 1814 in New York City of Irish parentage, Crawford moved to Rome in 1835. He remained there for the rest of his life. His non-portrait works freely expressed allegorical neo-classical motifs from mythology like this statue.

General John A Rawlins in Rawlins Park (1872)

General Grant's aide-de-camp throughout the Civil War, close personal friend and first Secretary of War, this bronze portrait statue was commissioned soon after his death in 1869. First erected in Rawlins Park at 18th and E streets NW, it led a peripatetic existence before returning to its first home in his namesake park.

The sculptor Joseph A Bailey was born in Paris in 1825; after service in the French Army during the Revolution of 1848, he immigrated to Philadelphia. In 1850, He trained there as well as in England. He is mainly noted for his statues in the Philadelphia area.

General James McPherson in McPherson Square (1876)

One of the first of the major Civil War generals to be honored, the statue was erected in 1876 sponsored by his comrades from the Army of the Tennessee that he had led in the Atlanta Campaign. It was cast in bronze taken from Confederate cannon captured during that campaign when he had met his death in 1864. Its dedication was led by Generals Sherman and Logan, his comrades in the Army of the Tennessee.

Its sculptor was Louis Rebisso Italian-born in 1837. He was forced to leave in 1857 because of his participation in Guiseppe Mazzini's "Young Italy" movement dedicated to republican principles.

Abraham Lincoln the Emancipator at Lincoln Square (1876)

This unique expression of Lincoln the Emancipator in Washington was conceived and funded in gratitude by those freed.

On the 11th anniversary of his assassination on April 14th 1876, Frederick Douglass was the lead orator at its dedication attended by President Grant, members of Congress and the Supreme Court and a mainly Negro crowd of 50,000. It was widely considered an expression of Negro attitude and gratitude despite the emphasis Douglass paid to Lincoln in his speech as the president of the whites with the Negro merely his "step-children."

Lincoln with the Emancipation Proclamation in his hand stands above the kneeling man with clearly African features breaking free, said to be the likeness of a man called Archer Alexander. Alexander was actually a man who escaped from slavery in Missouri and was saved from the effects of the still existing Fugitive Slave Law only by the protection of the anti-slavery Federal Army area commander. In actuality, his freedom was not achieved under the Emancipation Proclamation which freed only slaves in states that were "in rebellion" thus excluding Missouri. Although the right hand of the kneeling figure ends with a fist, the relationship between the two figures and the relative passivity of the Negro was part of the reigning iconography. Douglass noted the absence of a standing figure that might have signified equality and "manliness."

The sculptor was Thomas Ball. Born in Charlestown Massachusetts in 1819, he was apprenticed to a wood carver. Following 1854, he lived in the artistic colony in Florence Italy for most of the rest of his long life. He is primarily noted for the equestrian statue of George Washington in Boston's Public Gardens.

The Peace Monument at Pennsylvania Avenue and 1st Street (1877)

Better known as the Navy Monument, it was designed by Admiral David Dixon Porter to honor the sailors who died in the Civil War. A group of allegorical figures surround and surmount a four sided fountain.

The Anaconda Plan suggested by General Winfield Scott at the very start of the war envisaged a coastal naval blockade to prevent the importation of war supplies; to use the rivers to bisect the South while the very large army necessary to conquer the South was being trained. One of the major efforts of the Civil War thus involved the Union Navy from the start. The Navy's achievements were more central to the success of the Union than has been usually credited. These achievements required major changes in the operation of the Navy, the more traditional of the services. These changes were so far reaching as to change the course of future naval warfare no less than the changes induced by the actions of the Civil War on land warfare.

The Department of the Navy under Secretary Gideon Welles and Assistant Secretary Gustavus Fox organized a far larger Navy than had existed heretofore, unmatched until the build-up of the U.S. Navy in World War II. At the start, only forty-two ships were actually in commission, nineteen of which were sailing ships. The few ships available were mostly deep-draft and useless for coastal operation. Over the course of the war, the total number of ships increased from 90 to 670, ninety of which were ironclad. Its officers quintupled, its seamen more than sextupled and expenditures increased tenfold. A large number of the naval officers, including Matthew Maury, the Commander of the Naval Observatory, resigned to follow the Confederacy. It was therefore necessary to rebuild the navy entirely at the start of the war.

Like Lincoln and his generals, there was a sifting of the available naval commanders throughout the war to enable the ultimately victorious admirals to rise to the top. There was however not the same degree of experimenting that occurred in the army. By the end of 1862, Farragut was already on his way to becoming the first admiral in American history. He was successful already at New Orleans in 1862. Mobile remained open until the summer of 1864 when Farragut ran the gauntlet of the forts guarding Mobile Bay.

From the start of the war, the prime concern of Lincoln's Navy was to develop and maintain a tight blockade around the coast-line of the Confederacy. The success of the Navy in creating an early blockade of the

3500-mile Confederate coastline was unprecedented. One of the first of Lincoln's acts in the spring of 1861; at first merely a "paper" blockade; it was subject to criticism by other maritime powers. However, it succeeded in frightening off foreign shipping. A true blockade was in place by the end of 1861 and was one of the Union's highest priorities throughout the war.

Fortress Monroe at the mouth of Chesapeake Bay remained in Union hands. North Atlantic and South Atlantic Blockading Squadrons were established (demarcation along the border between the Carolinas) with the Hatteras Inlet and the newly conquered Port Royal near Hilton Head as a southerly coaling station. In addition, two Blockading Squadrons were eventually established for the Gulf ports (with New Orleans as its base after its capture in early 1862) and a Home Squadron in the West Indies. One hundred and eighty-nine harbors, openings to rivers or indentations were eventually guarded. On the Mississippi and its tributaries an additional 2000 miles were guarded.

In so doing, the Union Navy helped to carry out the ultimately successful "Anaconda" strategy recommended by General Winfield Scott. The blockade was effective in preventing the export of significant amounts of cotton to Europe. This hamstrung the Confederacy from having the resources necessary to carry on the war. In turn, there was preclusion of the import of the manufactured goods necessary to support the civilian population as well as the army. The South was deficient in industry; there were few iron-working establishments and no factory that could make marine engines. Particularly important was prevention of the importation of the heavy material needed to maintain the crucial railroad system. An additional result was the interdiction of the highly important coastal trade. This put a heavy burden on the inadequate railroads and added far higher costs to essential goods to be brought by land due to the use of ports inconvenient to the few through railroads. Particularly at risk was need for railroads to bring an adequate food supply for the Army of Northern Virginia and the burgeoning population of Richmond. Ultimately, this led to the proximal demise of the Confederacy.

General George H. Thomas at Thomas Circle (1879)

Donated by the Society of the Army of the Cumberland that he had led throughout the Civil War, its dedication in 1879 was one of the most highly attended following a large military parade and an encampment by the veterans of the Army of the Cumberland as a replication of the Grand Review of 1865.

Considered the finest equestrian statue in Washington, the sculptor was John Quincy Adams Ward. He was born in Urbana Ohio, a town founded by his grandfather. A member of the second generation of American sculptors, he trained in New York with Henry Kirke Brown rather than in Europe before setting up his own studio in 1861. Considered the greatest sculptor of his age, he was highly successful in designing monuments in Boston and New York as well as the equestrian statue of General Reynolds on the Gettysburg Battlefield killed at the start of hostilities.

Admiral David Farragut at Farragut Square (1881)

Figure 14 - Admiral David Farragut

Most noteworthy for its sculptress as well as is subject is that of Admiral Farragut at Farragut Square at Connecticut Ave and K Sts N.W. The Admiral is portrayed standing as if on a ship deck with his telescope ready in his hand. The statue was cast from the propeller of his flagship The *USS Hartford* at the Battle of Mobile Bay in 1864.

The sculptor was Vinnie Ream (later Hoxie), the first woman to receive a Federal commission. Born on the Wisconsin frontier in the 1840s, she first became famous for her bust of Lincoln from life just prior to his death in April 1865. Despite much opposition, she was later commissioned to do the life size Lincoln statue in the Capitol Rotunda. She was opposed in receiving that commission by the "radical" Republicans in the Congress intent on impeaching President Andrew Johnson. The apparently deciding vote preventing impeachment was cast by a senator she was accused as having influenced. She was later asked to do the statue of Farragut by his wife and aided in navigating the competitive political shoals by her friend General William Tecumseh Sherman.

Samuel DuPont at Dupont Circle (1884/1921)

Figure 15 - DuPont Fountain

Dupont Circle where Connecticut, Massachusetts, and New Hampshire Avenues meet with P St is a major traffic center. Its monument to Admiral Dupont is uniquely a fountain among the Civil War commanders. Its base contains three allegorical figures representing the Arts of Ocean Navigation, namely the male Wind, the female Sea and Goddess of the Stars. Descended from the famous Delaware munitions makers, his family provided in 1921 the fountain designed by Daniel Chester French, the sculptor of the seated Lincoln in his memorial. This very attractive fountain replaces an earlier less attractive bronze portrait of 1885.

The sculptor Daniel Chester French was born in Exeter New Hampshire, a neighbor and friend of Ralph Waldo Emerson and the Louisa May Alcott family. His first major commission was *The Minuteman* in Concord dedicated on April 19, 1875 in conjunction with the centennial of that battle. He also sculpted in 1884 the *John Harvard Monument* in the Harvard Yard as well as *Republic*, the centerpiece of Columbian Exposition of 1893. Wealthy and well-born, he epitomized the other "clubbable" members of the Commission of Fine Arts when he was appointed Chair in 1914 after the death of Daniel Burnham.

General Winfield Scott Hancock at Market Square (1896)

The heroic equestrian statue of General Winfield Scott Hancock was placed at Market Square at the halfway point in the Ceremonial Mile between the U.S. Capitol and the White House. The area received its name as the site of the important Center Market between 7th and 9th Streets adjoining the marshy side of the Mall and the Washington Canal (covered over in the 1870s to form B Street and finally Constitution Avenue). One of the original lots reserved by George Washington for the use of the United States Government in 1797, Center Market in 1802 was called "Marsh Market." One could shot ducks in this marshy area; the eastern portion of the Mall was always a soggy place.

After a fire in 1870, the old Market House was replaced in 1872 by an extensive building designed by Adolph Cluss, the leading architect in Washington at that time, also the architect of the Eastern Market at North Carolina Avenue on Capitol Hill. The center for streetcar lines, in the 1920s it was the largest retail market for fruits, vegetables and meat products. Its removal starting in 1928 was in preparation for the building of the Federal Triangle. The 8th Street Vista now looks north to the Patent Office on its knoll and south to the National Archives and the Hirschhorn Museum.

Born near Philadelphia in 1824, Hancock was assigned to the infantry after graduation for West Point in 1844. Named after the U.S. Army's commanding general, Hancock distinguished himself in the Mexican War under the command of his namesake in the campaign leading to the capture of Mexico City. He received the nickname of "Hancock the Superb" as a brigade commander in the Peninsula Campaign in the spring of 1862. He commanded a division in the II Corps at Antietam in September 1862 and continued under Hooker at Chancellorsville, the last in the spring of 1863 where he was wounded. At Gettysburg in July 1863, he was given command by General Meade of several army corps after the death early on July 1st of General Reynolds. Hancock took the lead in organizing the defenses on Cemetery Ridge. On the next day, despite a severe wound, his troops held the center of the line against attacks by A.P. Hill. Hancock also rallied his troops that bore the brunt of the charge on July 3rd by Pickett.

After recovering from his wounds, Hancock returned to command his II Corps during Grant's 1864 Overland Campaign distinguishing himself at the Battle of the Wilderness. After the war, his reputation as the Hero of

Gettysburg, his commitment to conservative constitutional principles and his conciliatory role during Reconstruction made him the Democratic Party nominee in 1880 against James Garfield. He lost by only several thousand votes but by a much larger margin in the Electoral College.

Dressed in the garb of a Civil War officer, he uniquely wears a broad brimmed square soft hat. The dedication ceremony in 1896 was attended by all the usual dignitaries. In recognition of his Democratic Party identity, President Grover Cleveland was the leading speaker, the only Democratic Party President during the entire post-Civil War era until 1912.

The sculptor was Henry Jackson Ellicott. Born in 1847 in Annapolis Maryland, he grew up in his family's home at Ellicott City and then Washington DC. He studied at the National Academy of Design under Constantino Brumidi among others. In 1889, he became Superintendant of the U.S. Treasury responsible for all Federal monuments.

General Ulysses S. Grant at Union Square (1900/1922)

General Grant was still in the Pantheon of American heroes in 1900. His Tomb on New York's Riverside Drive had but recently been completed after his highly attended New York funeral, the largest in American history. Although his presidency had been marred by scandal, he still remained the epitome of the unassuming "citizen-soldier" who had been commander of the victorious army. Instigated by the Society of the Army of the Tennessee of which he had been commander, the Grant Memorial Commission was set up in 1901 funded with $250,000 by Congress, the largest amount thus far. Proposals were elicited for a site just south of the State, War and Navy Building, parallel to the recently commissioned statue of General Sherman placed south of the Treasury.

Figure 16 - General Ulysses S. Grant

Secretary of War Elihu Root decided instead to coordinate the site of the Grant Memorial with the plans of the McMillan Commission. The overall theme of the expanded Mall projected by the McMillan Commission was to celebrate the victory of the Union in the Civil War. A Memorial to Grant was thought to be central to the monumental character of the expanded Mall along with a projected Lincoln Memorial and the existing Monument to Washington. The original suggestion of the Park Commission had been an arch dedicated to Grant at the head of the planned Memorial Bridge (now the site of the Lincoln Memorial) thus facing his military counterpart of the Lee Mansion crowning the Arlington National Cemetery.

Charles McKim, formerly on the McMillan Park Commission, was placed on the Advisory Board of the Grant Memorial along with other past McMillan Commission members such as Daniel Burnham and Augustus Saint-Gaudens. Contrary to the original proposal near the State, War and Navy Building, McKim now proposed a far more important role for a

Grant Memorial. Three large equestrian statues were to form a plaza arrangement at a site at the foot of the U.S. Capitol. This was envisaged to become a focal point at the eastern head of the Mall, to be called "Union Square" analogous to La Place de la Concorde in Paris in its significance.

The accepted design of Henry Merwin Shrady and Edward Pearce Casey was of Grant as a military figure flanked by Generals Sheridan and Sherman who had helped him to win the war. The entire ensemble was to function as a military reviewing stand. When actually built as the largest memorial in the city, its height is just short of the height of the contemporaneous Monument to Victor Emmanuel in Rome. Grant is the quiet even taciturn central figure on horseback flanked by artillery and cavalry groups. His appearance reflected his strength in remaining calm and decisive in the midst of crisis. The adjacent figures portray war as demanding courage and sacrifice. Finally completed in 1922, ultimately the Memorial as now placed with its reflecting pool at the confluence of Maryland and Pennsylvania Avenues (covering the freeway) fails to realize the aims fought over so bitterly to be an important addition to the design of the Mall.

The sculptor Henry Merwin Shrady was born in New York in 1871 to a socially prominent medical family. He graduated from Columbia University in 1894 and attended its law school before finally deciding on a career in art. An unknown, he received the commission for the Grant Memorial that had been highly sought by more established sculptors. Shrady discarded the earlier design. He spent the subsequent years in anatomical study to assure authenticity in his depiction of the straining horses in his equestrian groups. He literally poured his life into this work, dying as it was finished.

General John A. Logan at Logan Circle at 13th Street and Vermont Avenue (1901)

The statue was sponsored once again by the very active Society of the Army of the Tennessee; General John A Logan was for a short time its commander following the death of General McPherson in the Atlanta Campaign. Moreover, Logan was a commander of both the Society of the Army of the Tennessee and the Grand Army of the Republic (GAR). The latter was the politically potent veterans' organization that elected a roll call of Republican presidents from Grant to McKinley while also successfully advocating for generous veterans' pensions.

Franklin Simmons, the sculptor, created a massive statue that reflects the determination of the man. Born in Webster Maine in 1839, Simmons grew up in Bath and Lewiston. He attended Bates College in 1858. Moving to Washington during the Civil War, he was prolific in sculpting members of Lincoln's cabinet and military officers as well as some of the figures in Statuary Hall of the U.S. Capitol.

The pedestal is unique in its sculptured character designed by Richard Morris Hunt, the dean of Americans trained at L'Ecole des Beaux-Arts. One relief shows the General at a Council of War; the other his being sworn in as a Senator by the presiding vice-president that was historically inaccurate.

General George McClellan at Connecticut Avenue and Columbia Road (1902/1907)

Sponsored by some of his faithful soldiers, on a commanding height but on a small parklet far from the other Civil War generals, sits the nine-foot tall equestrian statue of General George McClellan. Commanding General of the United States Army for a short time in 1861-1862, he was also the commander of the Army of the Potomac from the summer of 1861 shortly after the debacle of the 1st Battle of Bull Run until November 1862. Primarily responsible for organizing the raw recruits into the formidable Army of the Potomac, he planned and executed the ultimately unsuccessful Peninsular Campaign in the spring of 1862 designed to capture the Confederate capital of Richmond. Deposed from command after the 2nd Battle of Bull Run, he was reinstated by Lincoln on the eve of the Battle of Antietam in September 1862.

He was finally deposed in the fall of 1862 for failing to pursue Robert E Lee's Army of Northern Virginia after his victory at Antietam but also for his disagreement with Lincoln's decision to issue the Emancipation Proclamation and change the political aims of the war. As a Democrat, McClellan stood for president in the election of 1864 in particular opposition to the policies of President Lincoln that might lead to racial equality.

The sculptor Frederick MacMonnies was chosen in a competition during the spring of 1902 judged by Charles Follen McKim, Daniel Chester French and Augustus Saint-Gaudens, the last one of his teachers. It is hardly surprising the statue and particularly its ornate pedestal strongly reflect the influence of the sculptor's training at the L'Ecole-des-Beaux Arts in Paris.

William Tecumseh Sherman at 15th Street and Pennsylvania Avenue (1903)

The top of Pennsylvania Avenue and 15th Street just south of the U.S. Treasury is the site of the very high equestrian Sherman Monument installed in 1903. The 1865 Grand Review is re-enacted by this site at the head of the Ceremonial Mile where, on its second day, General Sherman took the salute of his Army of the Tennessee. He chose not to join the other dignitaries at the reviewing stand at the White House where Secretary

145

of War Stanton also sat. The two men had differences about the lenient terms that Sherman had offered at the time of surrender of General Joseph E Johnston and his troops in North Carolina after the surrender of the Army of Northern Virginia by General Lee at Appomattox.

Born in Ohio in 1820; after the early death of his father, Sherman was raised in the family of Thomas Ewing, later also his father-in-law and an influential senator. Sherman graduated from West Point in 1840 and was assigned to the artillery. He was unusual in not seeing combat duty in the Mexican War but carried out administrative duties in California. At the start of the Civil War, Sherman was teaching at a military school in Louisiana that later became Louisiana State University. Although offered a commission by the Confederates, he joined the Union.

After service at Vicksburg, he was appointed by his friend Grant as his successor as commander of the Army of Tennessee. Sherman then carried out the famous March to the Sea through Georgia that became a model of modern war and its "scorched earth" policy. Successor to Grant as commander of the U.S.Army during the Reconstruction era, no friend of the newly freed, Sherman opposed continued use of the Army to enforce Reconstruction after 1876. He was also adamant about his refusal to enter politics.

Other generals who fought with Sherman in his capture of Atlanta are commemorated on his monument including medallions of General James McPherson and John A. Logan, otherwise also commemorated on their own monuments elsewhere in Washington. There are also two elaborate bronze groups depicting "War" and "Peace" and standing soldiers each representing the infantry, cavalry, artillery and engineers.

General Phillip Sheridan at Sheridan Circle (1908)

The westernmost of the equestrian statues is actually beyond the original boundary of the City of Washington at Sheridan Circle at 23rd St and Massachusetts Avenue N.W. Surrounded by embassies, General Philip Sheridan, the cavalry leader, is shown in his role of rallying his troops to win in 1864 at the Battle of Cedar Creek near Winchester in the Shenandoah Valley of Virginia. No less than the figure of the general is the rendition of his horse Rienzi as they together came to good effect to rally his troops. The statue was unveiled in 1908 by the general's son Lieutenant Phillip Sheridan in the presence of President Theodore Roosevelt.

By Gutzon Borglum, it was one of that sculptor's early triumphs in competition with John Quincy Adams Ward. Born in Idaho, Borglum grew up in Nebraska, and studied with Rodin in Paris. He dealt with figures of gigantic scale and nationalist themes as evidenced by his heroic presidential figures on Mount Rushmore commemorating Manifest Destiny.

George Stephenson and the GAR at 7th Street and Indiana Avenue (1909)

Figure 17 - The GAR Memorial

One of the less conspicuous memorials of the Civil War was also one of the last erected. It came as the Grand Army of the Republic (GAR) was winding down its membership and its influence as a potent political force. Inspired by the GAR, by 1890 "Decoration Day," had become a holiday in every northern state, monuments graced by the common soldier appeared in every town square and local burying grounds and battlefields. The GAR helped elect the entire roll call of Republican Party presidents from Grant to McKinley who had seen service in the Civil War. Theodore Roosevelt (TR), elected on his own in 1904, was the first president since 1868 that did not have Civil War credentials. Indeed, to the eternal shame of his warlike son, TR's father had opted out of the war by buying a substitute.

From the time of its founding until its height in the 1890s, the GAR became a very large organization of honorably discharged Union veterans and voters. By reflecting the characteristics of the generation of men mainly native-born who had fought in the Civil War, it helped maintain a sense of commitment to order, rank and exclusionary "national values" in the face of the nation's increased diversity.

After reaching a low in the 1870s, after the 1880s the GAR began aggressively to lobby Congress for liberalization of pensions. The original

1862 Pension Act had provided pensions to those injured in line of duty; and to the widows and orphans of those who died. In 1879, an "Arrears Act" provided arrears in a lump sum merely based on an affidavit rather than medical records and dated from the time of discharge or death rather than the time a pension had been granted. The substantial amounts thus available brought about a flood of pension applications, now encouraged by the more highly organized GAR.

The closeness of the popular vote between the two parties in the 1880s made the "soldier vote" even more important. At its height in the 1890s, the GAR enrolled almost 40% of all living Civil War veterans. It had achieved by the Pension Act of 1890 pensions to veterans, regardless of source of disability. All those who were "disabled from manual labor"; and thus practically all veterans merely based on age, could receive pensions regardless of income. Pensions were a right based on "service" rather than "dependency." Pensions became a major Federal expenditure.

The Stephenson Grand Army of the Republic Memorial is a granite shaft dedicated to the founder of the GAR. On its west side is a soldier and sailor in Civil War uniforms, symbolizing "Fraternity"; on the southeast side a woman with a sword symbolizing "Loyalty"; and on the northeast side a woman with a child symbolizing "Charity". There is also a medallion portrait of George Stephenson, a physician in the Union army in the 14th Illinois Regiment who organized the first post in Decatur Illinois. The date of its founding in April 1866 was the anniversary of the Battle of Shiloh in 1862 in which many of the first members had fought. In addition to its sense of fraternity and charity, another factor in its founding was the support that could be provided to the senatorial candidacy of former General John A. Logan, who became its commander-in-chief. After the 1880s, its power pointed to the very large Federal Pension Bureau Building that was built upon nearby 4th and F Streets.

The sculptor John Massey Rhind was born in Edinburgh Scotland in 1860. He studied at the Royal Scottish Academy, in London and then Paris. Immigrating to the United States in 1889, he settled in New York City. His reputation was established based on his winning a competition in 1890 to design one of the memorial doors at the Trinity Church in honor of John Jacob Astor II.

Abraham Lincoln in the Lincoln Memorial in West Potomac Park (1922)

Figure 18 – Abraham Lincoln

After his death on Good Friday in 1865, Lincoln had become the Christ-like martyr evoked periodically at election time by the Republican Party. Yet no major memorial to Lincoln had yet appeared commensurate to his importance to the history of the country. In the 1890s, the theme was to stress that which Americans of both North and South had in common. The Republican Party was firmly in control following McKinley's 1896 election. There had followed a strong presidency under Theodore Roosevelt. Honoring Lincoln at the centennial of his birth in 1909 would be as the strong Civil War president, and an even greater deification, but now as a titanic but humane "Man of the People."

The McMillan Commission offered the opportunity to create a Memorial at the west end of the expanded Mall commensurate with and directly in line with that of Washington's Monument and the U.S. Capitol. At the beginning, Charles McKim had visualized a standing figure of Lincoln silhouetted in front of a temple with a Doric columned portico in the center of a "rond-point." This memorial connecting the North and South via the Memorial Bridge to the Lee Mansion in Arlington National Cemetery could be compared with the Arc de Triomphe crowning La Place d"Etoile in Paris.

The original Lincoln Memorial Commission set up in 1902 was met headlong with delays and the opposition of Joseph Cannon, now the Republican Speaker of the House. Cannon was adamant in his opposition to the placement of the Memorial in West Potomac Park, land recently made by dredging the Potomac River. Furthermore, Cannon could not forgive McMillan for having bypassed him and the House of Representatives when setting up his Park Commission.

The removal of Cannon from his Speakership permitted the establishment in 1910 of the U.S.Commission of Fine Arts (CFA) "to advise upon statues, fountains and monuments." A new Lincoln Memorial Commission was quickly organized chaired by President Taft that deferred to the Fine Arts Commission and its not unforeseen choice of the site in West Potomac Park. One persistent alternative was for a highway from Washington to Gettysburg to be called the "Lincoln Highway," a name eventually used to designate the main national north-south road. Part of the urgency in 1910 was recognition that the Republican control of Congress was in jeopardy and the Democrats were far less likely to establish a memorial to a Republican President.

The CFA selected Henry Bacon as Architect for the Lincoln Memorial. Bacon had worked for Charles McKim and served as his representative on the 1893 Columbian Exposition before founding his own firm. Bacon's last project, it is a Greek temple reminiscent of the Parthenon but without its pediments. The use of the exterior Doric order and the interior Ionic order replicates that followed by the original. The statue within is visible from one of the sides of the building rather than from the front as in the Parthenon. The names of the states in the Union at the time of Lincoln's death are inscribed in the frieze above the 36 Doric columns with festoons of the 48 states on the attic representing the states at the time of the Memorial's completion.

At the time of the dedication of the memorial in 1922, Lincoln was clearly the symbol of reunion rather than the Republican northern hero of emancipation. He had become the god-like larger than life "preserver of the Union." The speakers made few if any references to the Civil War and the few grizzled veterans were from both sides. It may then not be surprising that there was segregated seating of the audience and only a single Negro speaker. Robert Moton was Booker T. Washington's successor at Tuskegee Institute, a Republican and an "accommodationist" in the tradition of his predecessor. His speech alluded to the delicate topic of the tension in American society between its principle of liberty and that of bondage. As the only reference to slavery, it was ignored by the press. The dedication was a microcosm of its times when the Ku Klux Klan paraded openly down Pennsylvania Avenue and lynchings occurred each year throughout the South.

In darkened light like a mausoleum, the huge seated statue by Daniel Chester French is enshrined like a god on a throne-like seat but realistically dressed. The image engrosses most visitors. Somber and pensive, he is the very image of a martyr who had to suffer the tragic flaw of slavery the Founders had left in the Constitution. Yet the words are also important. The statue is flanked in adjacent rooms by his *Gettysburg Address* and the *Second Inaugural Address*. In the first, he invoked the Declaration of Independence as the touchstone of the American experiment and emphasized that American democracy also must include equality. In the latter, he used Biblical phrases of mutual guilt for a plea for "binding wounds" and reconciliation. Prominently displayed on the arms of the chair and elsewhere are the Roman "fasces," a bundle of rods bound around a battle axe, traditionally a symbol of authority and justice but also of unity.

Completing the symbolism of reconciliation is the Memorial Bridge by the firm of McKim, Mead and White replicating a Roman aqueduct connecting the Lincoln Memorial to the Custis-Lee Mansion, home of Robert E. Lee and the Arlington National Cemetery. Indeed a very tall Confederate Soldiers Monument had been placed in Arlington National Cemetery in 1914. The sculptor Moses Jacob Ezekiel was born in Richmond to a Jewish family of Sephardic origin. He fought as a young cadet in the Confederate army before graduating from Virginia Military Institute (VMI) and remained an unreconstructed Confederate. Funded by the United Daughters of the Confederacy, the dedication was witnessed by President Wilson, a son of the South. The theme of the speakers was that of its times, mainly the spirit of common sacrifice and a common glorious future.

General George Gordon Meade at 3rd Street and Pennsylvania Avenue (1927)

George Meade was born in Cadiz Spain in 1815 of American parents and grew up in Philadelphia. He graduated from West Point in 1835 and was first assigned to the artillery and recognized for bravery in the Mexican War. He worked as a civilian engineer for a time before returning to the army in 1842. He spent the years prior to the Civil War mainly in building lighthouses including the Absecon Light at Atlantic City. His Civil War career was as a brigade commander under McClellan in the Peninsular Campaign; as a corps commander at South Mountain and Antietam where he distinguished himself. He fought, again at Fredericksburg and Chancellorsville under Generals Burnside and Hooker before being given command of the Army of the Potomac on the eve of the Battle of Gettysburg in July 1863.

He is credited with winning that important battle but blamed for failing to pursue Lee immediately after. His command of the Army of the Potomac for the rest of the war was overshadowed by the direct involvement of the Commanding General Ulysses Grant in that theater of the war. Meade's somewhat tarnished military reputation and the mutual dislike of the journalists attached to the army perhaps contributed to his relative obscurity and the long delay in the placement of his statue as well as its allegorical non-equestrian theme.

The bare headed figure of Meade stands in front of a brutal figure of "War" in the rear with massive wings that engulf the three mainly nude figures on either side representing the various positive qualities possessed by Meade. A son of Pennsylvania, the monument was commissioned by the Pennsylvania State Legislature and carried out by a Philadelphia sculptor Charles Grafly. Grafly taught at the Pennsylvania Academy of Fine Arts and was an expert in interpreting the French allegorical sculpture of the late 19th and early 20th century which this monument represents.

One of the last of the Civil War Memorials of military figures, it was dedicated by President Coolidge in 1927 as part of an elaborate ceremony with military bands and speeches that extolled the veterans of the Union forces that fought at Gettysburg.

The Spirit of Freedom at 10th and U Streets (1997)

The Grand Review on Pennsylvania Avenue in May 1865 did not include any units that represented the nearly 180,000 Black soldiers and their 7000 White officers that fought during the Civil War. Unlike portraying emancipation as a passive act, these men had fought for their own liberation. At the celebration of the unveiling of the African-American Civil War Memorial in September 1996, 300 Blacks in Civil War Union uniforms marched down Pennsylvania Avenue in a reenactment of that 1865 Grand Review from which their ancestors had been omitted.

As early as the summer of 1861, escaped slaves began to appear at Union lines at places like Fortress Monroe. The Union commander Benjamin Butler determined that they would be considered as "contraband" of war and used as laborers rather than be returned to their owners under the still extant Fugitive Slave Law. As Union forces entered the Confederacy, an increasing number of slaves sought freedom. Although authorized by the Second Confiscation Act in July 1862, the various efforts taken during 1862 by union commanders to recruit slaves as armed troops were rejected by Lincoln. Authorization occurred with the actual issuance of the Emancipation Proclamation to take effect on January 1st 1863. This was followed in the spring by active recruitment of "Colored" troops. The movie *Glory* in the early 1990s brought attention to the battle at Fort

Wagner in Charleston Harbor in July 1863 in which Robert Gould Shaw and his Colored 54th Massachusetts Regiment fought bravely and incurred heavy losses.

Built at 10th and U Streets N.W., the African-American Civil War Memorial is in the midst of the African-American "Shaw" neighborhood adjacent to Howard University named after what had been the local Robert Gould Shaw Public School. "The Spirit of Freedom" hovers over larger than life figures with African features of three armed soldiers and a sailor holding a ship's wheel. In the mode of post-modern monuments, it also lists the names of the approximately 200,000 persons involved in the Civil War.

The sculptor Ed Hamilton was born in 1947 in Cincinnati Ohio grew up and continues to live in Louisville Kentucky. He graduated from the Louisville School of Art in 1969 and has taught in the Louisville Public Schools and at Jefferson Community College.

Martin Luther King Jr Memorial at Independence Avenue and Tidal Basin (2011)

Figure 19 – Martin Luther King Jr. Memorial

Situated on the Tidal Basin within sight of the Lincoln Memorial and the Jefferson Memorial is Washington's most recent memorial. It reflects the struggle that has occurred to implement the promise of the Civil War. One walks on a path through a divided large stone boulder called the "Mountain of Despair" symbolic of the long civil rights struggle. One is led to a "Stone of Hope" from which the 28 foot standing figure of Martin Luther King emerges. Surrounding are inscriptions of quotations from his writings and speeches.

The goals derived from the abolition of slavery in the 13th Amendment of 1865, of equal rights in the 14th Amendment in 1867 and of voting rights in the 15th Amendment in 1870 had been held in abeyance by terrorism and legal restrictions imposed after the failure of Reconstruction in the 1870s. The one hundredth anniversary of the Emancipation Proclamation and the Gettysburg Address in 1963 was an opportunity to renew that promise.

In August 1963 over 200,000 persons assembled at the Lincoln Memorial. The most remembered protest in the history of the United States, it was part of what had been local actions throughout the south that had combined "the rhetoric of Christian expectations and American democracy with tactics of Gandhi's nonviolent direct action," Huge numbers came. For example, as many as 450 busloads arrived from New York City. Since the 1939 concert by Marian Anderson, the Lincoln Memorial had begun to stand for Lincoln the Emancipator. Now, for the first time since Reconstruction, the principle of racial justice could find widespread support by Whites as well as Blacks. .

The modern civil rights movement is conventionally defined by the start of the Montgomery bus boycott in December 1955. Rosa Parks, an official of the Alabama NAACP, refused to move to the rear of the bus as required under segregation custom and law. Martin Luther King Jr, (MLK) recently appointed Baptist pastor to a church in Montgomery, led the boycott. After over a year, the boycott achieved the desegregation of the buses. In 1957, King formed the Southern Christian Leadership Conference (SCLC) to continue civil rights protests.

Nevertheless, there was no further civil rights action until 1960. In February, four students from North Carolina A&T in Greensboro North Carolina sat-in at a segregated Woolworth lunch counter. The movement spread to Nashville where there were several Black colleges and then elsewhere. Formed soon after, the members of the Student Non Violent Coordinating Committee (SNCC) by their egalitarianism and non-violence were also challenging their elders and the hierarchy of the black churches.

President John Kennedy's inaugural address of January 1961 that spurred Americans to a new activism did not mention civil rights. Yet on the next day, James Meredith made his application to admission to the University of Mississippi Law School. During the spring and summer of 1961 under the sponsorship of the Congress of Racial Equality (CORE), the mainly young inter-racial Freedom Riders confronted failure to implement the right granted by the Supreme Court since 1946 to integrate the interstate buses and the bus stations in the South.

154

When the Freedom Riders started in the spring of 1961, they had not yet aroused much popular support. The Department of Justice under Attorney General Robert Kennedy (RFK), the president's brother and close political adviser, was concerned about the risk with buses being burned, about the possibility of violence, of people being killed, but also of losing control. Litigation was their métier by which the federal government chose to enforce the actions of the Supreme Court leading to contempt of court citations; and in relatively rare instances and for relatively short periods, the use of armed force by the several hundred federal marshals available as needed.

Despite the mobs who attacked them; and then the police who arrested them, more students continued to ride the buses. The pictures of burned buses spread throughout the world by television were detrimental to the image of the United States in its propaganda battle with the Soviet Union. RFK brokered an agreement to call off the rides in response to bringing the Interstate Commerce Commission (ICC) to act. Finally, in September 1961, the ICC acted to outlaw segregation in interstate transportation. What had been avoided for so many years and could have awaited additional years of legal delay was resolved rapidly on a moral direct action basis.

The next confrontation that came dramatically in front of the television cameras was the "interposition" of the Governor of Mississippi in September 1962 to the entry of James Meredith to the University of Mississippi Law School. Meredith's entry had been prepared for long in advance. The federal marshals were there to escort him but the mob was far too large. The Mississippi National Guard was federalized. The 101st Airborne Division was slow in coming but did come. The situation seemed to many a fiasco.

1963 was the 100th anniversary of the Emancipation Proclamation. Yet the Civil Rights movement was stalled. Whereas RFK saw the goal as a pragmatic political one to increase registration where it was indeed possible to accomplish easily, King wanted to go to where no registration was possible to arouse the conscience of the nation and create a dramatic confrontation. Birmingham in Alabama was chosen by Martin Luther King to be the site in May 1963 for the beginning of what became the Children's Crusade of young children marching for civil rights. They were met by Police Chief Eugene "Bull" Connor's men with their K-9 dogs and water hoses in full view of the world. Thousands of the young people were imprisoned but more came on successive days. 30,000 troops were encamped around the city and a thoroughgoing desegregation agreement was made in Birmingham, "the most segregated city in the South."

Shortly thereafter in June, George Wallace, the Alabama governor, carried out his threat "to stand in the schoolhouse door" to prevent the entry of two Negro students to the University of Alabama. This time, the troops were already nearby but it was merely a charade; no violence occurred, the students were quietly admitted escorted by Department of Justice officials and Wallace withdrew.

On the evening of June 11th, Kennedy made his famous speech invoking the full support of the federal government for desegregation as a moral crusade; and his plan to submit a civil rights bill to Congress in the teeth of the power of its control by the Southerners. Kennedy spoke about "the events in Birmingham and elsewhere have so increased the cries for equality that no legislative body can *prudently* [emphasis added] choose to ignore...we face therefore a moral crisis as a country." That same night, Medgar Evers, the head of the NAACP and organizer of voter registration in Mississippi, was killed. In September, a bomb killed four young girls at Birmingham's Sixteenth Street Baptist Church.

The August 1963 March on Washington had the wary cooperation of the Kennedy Administration and invited the participation of white union and religious leaders. Martin Luther King made his *I Have a Dream* speech on the steps of the Lincoln Memorial that reaffirmed his belief in the ultimate redemption of the words in the Declaration of Independence and the U.S. Constitution. Civil Rights had achieved national moral stature in the shadow of Abraham Lincoln.

The success of this March in terms of its numbers and the inspirational speech of MLK set the tone for many future protests. The Civil Rights Bill assuring equal rights in accommodation was eventually passed under President Lyndon Johnson in June 1964 as a first step in the Second Reconstruction. More protests were necessary including the 1965 March from Selma to Montgomery Alabama before voting rights were achieved. Martin Luther King won the Nobel Peace Prize and went on to expand his ministry to the larger area of rights of the poor and the Viet Nam War before his assassination at Easter 1968. His presence now in the sacred ground of the Tidal Basin in view of both the Lincoln Memorial and the Jefferson Memorial recognizes his great stature in helping to realize the promise of the Civil War.

CHAPTER 9
THE WARS OF THE 20TH CENTURY

The rise of the United States to world stature in the 20th century, "The American Century", brought it into the great World Wars and the Cold War that followed after World War II. The streets of Washington began to reflect not only the triumph of American arms but of those international figures that identified with the spirit that America represented of political freedom and individual liberty.

9.1 World War I

The 1st Division Monument at President's Park South (1924/1957)

The 80 foot Massachusetts granite column, one of the largest ever quarried, is surmounted by a gilded winged statue of Victory carrying a flag. The monument was first dedicated in 1924 by President Calvin Coolidge in the presence of General John J Pershing. Designed by Daniel Chester French, the sculptor of Abraham Lincoln in the Lincoln Memorial, it also lists the names of the nearly 6000 members of the First Division in the American Expeditionary Force (AEF) who died in France during World War I. An exedra added after World War II contains the names of the nearly 4500 men of that division killed during World War II.

Known as "The Big Red", the 1st Division was organized in New York in June 1917, reached its full strength of 27,000 men in August and first entered combat in France in October 1917. In April 1918, with the Germans only 40 miles from Paris, the 1st Division captured the hill at Cantigny, and then in July, the important town of Soissons at high cost. In September 1918, the 1st division helped clear the St Mihiel Salient and then, in its last battle, the Meuse-Argonne Forest. At the end of the war, it had reached Sedan, the furthest penetration of American forces and the rail center supporting the German lines that was the objective of that last offensive. It had suffered 23,000 casualties and became known by the gallows humor of its men as "The Big Dead One."

During World War II, the 1st Division was redesignated in May 1942, landed in England in August, and took part in the amphibious assault on French North Africa on 8th November 1942. In continuous combat from January to May 1943, it helped secure Tunisia. In July 1943, it was part of General George Patton's force in the invasion of Sicily and fought at high cost to capture its mountains. Returned to England, it was in the first wave on Omaha Beach on 6th June 1944 suffering 30% casualties. participated in the breakthrough at St Lo and the drive across France capturing Aachen Germany in October 1944. After action in repelling the German attack in the Battle of the Bulge in the Ardennes Forest in December 1944, the 1st Division reached Czechoslovakia before the end of the war in May 1945. It suffered nearly 20,000 casualties while earning fifteen Medals of Honor.

The Tomb of the Unknown Soldier at Arlington National Cemetery (1931)

The pristine white marble draped figures and the Doric pilasters are reminiscent of an ancient Greek tomb. Within the tomb lies an unidentified American killed in France beneath the inscription "Here rests in honored glory an unknown American soldier known only to God." Subsequently on Memorial Day 1958, unknown dead soldiers from World War II and the Korean War were buried nearby

The tomb is guarded every day in the year for twenty-four hours each day by a specially trained unit of the 3rd U.S. Infantry Regiment (The Old Guard). The Amphitheater associated with the tomb is used for annual celebrations of Memorial Day and Veterans Day as well as the funeral of such as General of the Army John J Pershing.

The sculptor Thomas Hudson Jones was born in Buffalo in 1892 and trained at its Albright Art School. He worked with Daniel Chester French on his statue of Lincoln before taking up a fellowship at the American Academy in Rome where he also became Professor of Fine Arts in 1934. After 1944, he became associated with the Institute of Heraldry in Washington where he was responsible for the design of the insignia of the Air Force Academy and Army medals including the World War II Victory Medal.

The District of Columbia World War I Memorial in West Potomac Park near Independence Avenue (1931)

Figure 20 – District of Columbia WWI Memorial

The domed peristyle Doric Greek temple is in the style of its era exemplified by the contemporary Tomb of the Unknown Soldier at Arlington National Cemetery. Dedicated by President Herbert Hoover on Armistice Day 1931, it lists the names of the 26,000 who served and the nearly 500 who died from the District of Columbia. .

Mariners Memorial at George Washington Memorial Parkway (1934)

Figure 21 - Mariners Memorial

Seven gulls hovering over a breaking wave honor the sailors, both military and civilian, who died at sea during World War I. A dynamic and evocative sculpture, it was made of what was then unusual metal of aluminum. The original plan to have a stepped base of green granite to simulate the sea has never been realized.

The Second Division Memorial at Constitution Avenue and 18th Street (1936/1962)

The fiery gilded bronze sword in the center guards the route to Paris in honor of the men of the Second Division in World War I. It is complemented by wings added to the west of World War II and to the east of the Korean War.

Figure 22 - Second Division Monument

At its first dedication in 1936, President Franklin Roosevelt paid his respects to "the splendid achievements of the Second Division." Constituted in September 1917, the "Indian Head Division" contained a Marine Brigade along with several U.S. Army regiments. It was unique among army units in having several U.S. Marine officers serving as division commanders. It entered combat in France in the Battle of Belleau Wood in the spring of 1918 to prevent the German advance to Paris, fought at Soissons before taking part in the final Battle of the Meuse-Argonne. There were approximately 22,000 casualties, half Marines. It took part in the occupation of Germany until its return to the States in 1924.

The Second Division was unusual in remaining intact as an organization during the interwar era. It landed at Belfast and was stationed in England in preparation for the invasion. After landing on Omaha Beach on June 8th, 1944, it participated in the St Lo breakthrough to capture Brest, the heavily defended U-boat base in western France, After helping to stop the German Ardennes offensive in December 1944, the Second division reached the Rhine in March 1945, captured Gottingen and Leipzig in April before reaching Pilsen in Czechoslovakia by V-E Day in May 1945. It was in training for the invasion of Japan when V-J Day occurred in August 1945.

The sculptor James Earle Fraser, born in Winona Minnesota in 1876, was one of the most active in Washington during the 1930s. Trained at the Art Institute of Chicago and L'Ecole des Beaux-Arts in Paris, he was heavily influenced at first by his mentor Augustus Saint Gaudens. He is most famous for his Buffalo head nickel (1913) and his doleful *End of the Trail* in 1915.

John J. Pershing in Pershing Park at Pennsylvania Avenue and 15th Street (1979)

Figure 23- John J. Pershing

The long delayed recognition of the American commander in World War I is near the site of the temporary Triumphal Arch through which Pershing on a horse led the 1st Division in September 1919. In a wooded area, there is a standing figure of General Jack Pershing adjoining a relief showing the American advances on the Western Front in 1918. He fought at Wounded Knee, Cuba and the Philippines before leading the attack on Pancho Villa in Mexico in 1916. Appointed in 1917 commander of the American forces in World War I, he was given after his victory the extraordinary rank of "General of the Army," the first person so designated.

The sculptor Robert Winthrop White was born in 1921, the grandson of the architect Stanford White. He attended the Rhode Island School of Design and the American Academy at Rome. He taught at the State

University of New York at Stony Brook for most of his career. He was noted for his neo-classical portrait work.

9.2 World War II

The Marine Corps War Memorial at Arlington National Cemetery (1954)

Figure 24 - Marine Corps Iwo Jima Memorial

The first of the war memorials commemorating World War II, it replicates a famous Pulitzer prize-winning photo by Joe Rosenthal. A symbolic raising of the American flag occurred at the summit of the extinct volcano Mount Suribachi on Iwo Jima in February 1945. Iwo Jima was one of a series of Pacific islands hard-won from the Japanese in the drive to the conquest of Japan's Home Islands. After the American capture of islands in the Marshall and Mariana chains during 1944, Iwo Jima appeared to be next. Far closer to the Japanese mainland, it served as part of a system for the Japanese to warn of American bombers coming to the Home Islands. Its capture would also enable far better fighter plane cover for B-29 bomber raids. However, it was unexpectedly far more heavily fortified and staunchly defended; and relatively unaffected by the preceding intensive air and naval bombardment. Three Marine divisions took thirty-five days; over 6000 men died to rout the 22,000 Japanese soldiers from this strategic island.

The statue was funded by former Marines and other patriotic Americans. It incorporated the real faces of the men who had participated one of whom was a Pima Indian along with a pole and a real American flag that still flies continuously. The base is inscribed with the names of the Marine Corps engagements since 1775 and with the tribute by Fleet Admiral Nimitz to those who fought to conquer Iwo Jima "Uncommon Valor was a Common Virtue."

The sculptor Felix de Weldon was born in Vienna Austria in 1907 and eventually received his degree from the University of Vienna Academy of Creative Arts and School of Architecture. A prolific artist, he first came to North America to do a bust of Canadian Prime Minister Mackenzie King. He served in the United States Navy during World War II and became an American citizen in 1945. A member of the Commission of Fine Arts during the Eisenhower and Kennedy Administrations, he helped implement President Kennedy's 1963 directive to make Federal architecture more reflective of modernism.

The Netherlands Carillon at Arlington National Cemetery (1960)

Exemplary of the role of the United States as the leader of the Grand Coalition that liberated Europe is the monument north of Arlington National Cemetery. Commemorating the Liberation of Netherlands, the Netherlands Carillon and Tower recalls the ringing of bells throughout the country announcing the liberation from the Nazi German conquerors on V-E Day May 9 1945. The forty-nine bells were funded by the various areas of the country that then each was inscribed with the coat-of-arms or other insignia of that segment of the population. The rectangular steel frame tower holding the bells is reminiscent of the geometric work of the modernist Dutch painter Piet Mondrian.

Queen Juliana of the Netherlands first presented the bells to the people of the United States at the time of her state visit to Washington in 1952. During World War II, Juliana, the only child of the then Queen Wilhelmina, lived in exile with her children in Ottawa Canada. She succeeded her mother as Queen in 1948 just before accepting the independence of Indonesia, the former Dutch East Indies, and the jewel of their empire. Due to an infection with rubella during the pregnancy, one of her children was born with serious disabilities that led to Juliana's support for children with disabilities in the underdeveloped world.

Winston Churchill on Massachusetts Avenue (1966)

Figure 25 - Winston Churchill

With one foot on American soil and one foot on the British soil of its embassy, Winston Churchill symbolizes his dual parentage and his honorary United States citizenship but primarily his close relationship with President Franklin Roosevelt during World War II. The English Speaking Union funded this statue in furtherance of the Anglo-American "special relationship" that was so crucial to victory.

The statue shows the British Prime Minister at his greatest time with his fingers in the "V" for "Victory" and his ever-present cigar. The sculptor William Mozart McVey was born in Boston in 1905 but grew up in Cleveland Ohio. After training at the Cleveland School of Art, he lived in Paris. On the faculty of the University of Texas and Cranbrook Academy, he returned as a faculty member of the Cleveland Institute of Art for the major part of his career. His playfulness is illustrated by his animal sculptures elsewhere but also by his humanizing portrait of Churchill.

John F. Kennedy in the Kennedy Center for the Performing Arts (1971)

John F Kennedy (JFK) was the 35th president from January 1961 to November 1963 when he was assassinated in Dallas Texas. His assassination was never totally explained but in some way related to the preoccupation of the United States during his presidency with the existence of a Communist government in Cuba. His inaugural address in January 1961 issued a call for a commitment to an aggressive foreign policy in opposition to the influence of the Soviet Union. This policy led eventually to American military involvement in Viet Nam at the very periphery of American power.

The advent of the youthful and handsome John Kennedy to the presidency was a time of great confidence. In his famous inaugural address, the World War II war hero started by invoking the rise of a new generation; a generation forged in the crucible of the victorious war; the junior officers who had fought that war that brought the United States to the pinnacle of power. They were men in their forties like him who shared the conviction that the world might yield to their efforts; that "there was nothing we, or America, could not do."

Although JFK was himself bored with concerts and high culture, "Recognition of Excellence" of the arts was to be one of the themes of the Kennedy Administration. Although it had not originally intended, the Kennedy Administration thoroughly revised the federal attitude toward the arts, transforming national cultural policy from a special interest to a public concern. It was indeed to be a new Augustan age—a golden age of poetry and power that was connected with the romantic fantasy of the Arthurian legend of Camelot.

Beyond his planned recital of his poem *The Gift Outright*, Robert Frost was so delighted with the opportunity to participate in the Kennedy inaugural that he volunteered to compose a poem for the inauguration, an extraordinary commitment. His poem called *Dedication* spoke presciently of "the glory of a next Augustan age…a golden age of poetry and power" The story of the old man standing in the bright winter sun, unable to read the new poem but then reciting in his strong voice the poem he knew, set a human tone to the inauguration that nearly upstaged the strident presidential Cold War address.

In follow-up of this connection between Kennedy and the poet, Secretary of the Interior Stewart Udall began, with an "Evening with Robert Frost," at a black-tie affair at the State Department, the "President's Cabinet Artists Series." Over the next few years, fifteen such programs were presented that represented a wave of culture that became the new fashion. Carl Sandburg was a natural selection; Marian Anderson another and Thornton Wilder still another. The planned invitation to Pablo Casals was upstaged by his invitation to the White House.

Since World War II, repeated federal arts initiatives had failed. Cultural opponents had attacked federal arts support as a return to the "boondoggling" of the New Deal WPA. The common assumption was that the arts were "mere luxuries," even un-American. The entire Kennedy arts initiative changed the attitude of the country toward such seemingly arcane arts such as poetry and gave the country additional prestige abroad. In October 1963, before his departure for Dallas, in dedicating the Frost Library at Amherst, JFK linked art with the very creation of national values. The very individuality of the artist was essential to the strength of our civilization; ever the Cold Warrior, it was what distinguished us from our adversary.

JFK also re-opened the long stalled drive for building a National Cultural Center near the Lincoln Memorial along the Potomac River. There the initiative stood when his assassination interrupted any progress toward implementing these principles. In 1964, groundbreaking occurred by President Lyndon Johnson (LBJ) for a Center for the Performing Arts to be named for the martyred president. Also arising out of this evolution during the Kennedy years, in September 1965, LBJ signed legislation to establish the National Endowments for the Arts and the Humanities.

The greater than life-size bust of John Kennedy looks onto the center of the red carpeted Grand Foyer of the Kennedy Center that unites the three theaters it contains. The sculptor Robert Berks was also noted for his full size statue of Albert Einstein and the Mary McLeod Bethune statue in Lincoln Park.

The Navy Memorial at Pennsylvania Avenue and 7th Street (1987)

A fountain is surrounded by a neo-classical Doric semi-circle that leads to the 8th Street vista to the Doric Old Patent Office. There is a huge granite map of the planet Earth showing the predominance of its oceans. To the side is the solitary standing life-size Lone Sailor with his duffel bag representing all those who have served and will serve in the U.S. Navy. Along the sides are reliefs illustrating the great ships in the historical evolution of the Navy.

The Franklin Roosevelt Memorial on the Tidal Basin (1997)

Figure 26 – Franklin Delano Roosevelt in wheelchair

Following his death in April 1945, acting on his stated wishes, President Franklin Roosevelt's (FDR) only memorial was a marble slab "the size of my desk" in front of the National Archives Building on Pennsylvania Avenue. Considered by many as the greatest American president during both the Great Depression and World War II and the only one elected for more than two terms, he remained relatively unheralded. Although designed in 1978 before the Vietnam Veterans Memorial, the Roosevelt Memorial was completed only in 1997 during the Democratic Party presidency of William Jefferson Clinton.

The FDR Memorial lies along the Tidal Basin amidst the cherry trees in the sacred area between the Lincoln and Jefferson Memorials. A landscape rather than a structure, the Memorial is unique among Presidential Memorials in its extensive use of water and its use of four areas or rooms to denote his four terms in office, related also to the Four Freedoms mentioned in his speeches. There are four sequential spaces containing statues such as a "bread line" and other sculptural elements each separated by a stone "garden."

Illustrating the times in which he lived, it describes the early years of the crashing Depression with a single waterfall; multiple stair drops describes the public works such as the Tennessee Valley Authority; chaotic falls at varying angles denotes the chaos of World War II and a still pool his death. Only after some controversy, Roosevelt is shown using a wheelchair, never seen by the public during his time in office.

The landscape architect Lawrence Halprin was born in Brooklyn New York in 1916. He trained at Cornell and University of Wisconsin, where he came under the influence of Frank Lloyd Wright at Taliesin east and finally at the Harvard School of Design under Walter Gropius and Marcel Breuer. His classmates there included Philip Johnson and I.M. Pei. Living in San Francisco, he built fountains and landscapes that invited human participation.

The World War II Memorial on the National Mall (2004)

The definitive World War II Memorial on The National Mall was long delayed and contentious in its design and site. On the former site of the Rainbow Pool, it lies at the eastern end of the Reflecting Pool between the Lincoln Memorial and the Washington Monument. Its position in the monumental center of American patriotism recognizes its central position in the history of the United States in the 20th century. Considered by some as "vainglorious," it is clearly grand with rows of pillars and bi-axial symmetry in the tradition of far earlier neo-classical monuments.

The architect Frederich St Florian was born in 1932 in Graz Austria. He studied at the Graz Institute of Technology and Columbia University. A long-time member of the faculty of the Rhode Island School of Design, he claims professional descent from Mies van der Rohe and le Corbusier.

9.3 The Cold War and Beyond

The United States role as a world power and the leader of the free world post-World War II was translated into a series of wars. In the intervening generation of the "Cold War," two somewhat unsatisfactory wars were fought at great cost and at great distance at the periphery of American power in Korea and Viet Nam. The ambiguity of the results of these wars was reflected in the timing and the character of their memorials in the sacred precincts of Washington.

The Viet Nam Veterans Memorial on the Mall (1982)

Figure 27 - Viet Nam Veterans Memorial

Not an object but a landscape, the Viet Nam Veterans Memorial on the Mall most clearly reflects the ambiguity of the post-World War II American world hegemony. Unlike the previous wars that memorialized generals on horses, this lists the names of persons who died without reference to rank nor does it list the names of battles. Selected from over 1400 entries in the largest architectural competition in history, the "Wall" is funerary rather than triumphant or heroic. Its sculptor, then a young unknown Asian-American student at Yale, focuses on the more than fifty-seven thousand lives lost.

The American defense of South Viet Nam against a guerilla insurgency from its Communist North ultimately failed. Moreover, there had been disunion in the country over its morality and its value. Veterans returning from what was a very difficult war fought against guerrillas were not welcomed home. Military service was for some a mark of shame rather than the glory that had met the veterans of World War II and even Korea.

A group of Viet Nam veterans led by Jan Scruggs, a former enlisted man, created the Viet Nam Veterans Memorial on the Mall to redress these issues, to encourage national healing and reconciliation. Scruggs determined that all names are there and nothing distinguishes the rank of the dead. Controversy over its design and placement of the Memorial reflected the controversy over the war itself. One learns nothing about the war's cause or purpose because the cause and purpose were unclear. On entering the valley of the dead that the Vietnam Memorial Wall represents, the inscription is "1959 in honor of the men and women of the Armed Forces of the United States who served in the Vietnam War. The names of those who gave their lives and those who remain missing are inscribed in the order they were taken from us." The names and dates are inscribed on polished black granite that further contributes to the power of reflection that it creates. It ends with "1975 our nation honors the courage, service and devotion to duty and country of its Vietnam veterans…" The sentiment behind it is neither patriotic nor unpatriotic but an honoring of the boundary between the living and the dead that invites contemplation and participation from the visitor. A place of pilgrimage, visitors and family members place tokens and flowers along side the wall daily.

The sculptor Maya Lin was born in 1959 in Athens Ohio to recently arrived Chinese immigrants and whose family was on the art and architecture faculty at Ohio University. She describes her first work "I imagined a knife and cutting into the earth, opening it up, an initial violence and pain that in time would heal. The grass would grow back but the initial cut remains a pure flat surface in the earth with a polished mirrored surface." As a void in the earth, it represents those who died but also invites reflection on its polished granite from those who visit and leave flowers and other objects.

Tom Carhart, originally a member of the Viet Nam Veterans Memorial Commission, broke with his colleagues over the choice of Lin's design, calling it a "deep gash of shame." He and others demanded something more that indicated patriotism and reverence for the country. He led a group that commissioned Frederick Hart's *Three Infantrymen* just to the right of a high flagpole with the American flag placed at a slight distance from the Wall. One of the Infantrymen appears to be Caucasian, another African American and the third Hispanic to represent the racial diversity of the military. In addition, in 1994, the *Vietnam Women's Memorial* by Glenna Goodacre was added to honor the 8000 nurses who served in Viet Nam. It shows three nurses with one holding a soldier receiving help like the Madonna in the tradition of the Pieta. It is suggested that this amalgam of images has served to bring about the reconciliation that the Memorial sought to achieve by incorporating the commemorative wishes of several different segments of those interested.

The Korean War Memorial on the Mall (1995)

The Korean War had taken place many years before in the 1950s. However, The Korean War Veterans Memorial was not completed until

1995. Unlike World War II, there was no clear end point but merely a truce with a continued presence along the 38th parallel, nor were there any welcoming parades as individual soldiers returned home. The "police action" to protect South Korea from its neighboring Communist North Korea that took over 50,000 American lives seemed to fade into obscurity, to be "a forgotten war."

In the meantime, the Viet Nam War had taken place between 1965 and 1973 with a great deal of conflict in the country. The dedication of the Viet Nam Veterans Memorial in 1982 renewed interest in recognizing the veterans of the earlier war. Although there were several similarities including a dark wall on which there were faces of soldiers rather than names, there was clear need to provide some of the realism that the symbolic Vietnam Wall had initially avoided. Bronze soldiers as though on a night patrol celebrate the infantry man, the simple soldier. Their number of nineteen (doubled with their shadows on the wall) are symbolic of the thirty-eighth parallel that divides Korea. They form a triangle leading to a pool of water as does the peninsula of Korea jutting into the sea.

Unlike its neighbor on the Mall, it did not need to bring about reconciliation but just recognition. The Korean War did not divide the country. The United States fought as part of an international coalition under United Nations auspices. The Korean Veterans Memorial placed in a grove of trees in the shadow of the Lincoln Memorial and across the Reflecting Pool from the Viet Nam Veterans Memorial together create a sacred triangle of memorials in the west end of the Mall.

The themes of the Cold War were of freedom from oppression and anti-colonialism. The streets of Washington have served in many different instances to express this theme of anti-colonialism also reflecting their constituencies in the United States but now also did so also directly in opposition to the Soviet Union.

Robert Emmet at Massachusetts Avenue and 24th Street NW (1917)

He stands as he did at the time when sentenced to death in 1803 after having led an unsuccessful Irish revolt against the British. On the pedestal is his evocation of the example of the American George Washington. "I wished to procure for my country the guarantee that Washington procured for America."

Funded by Americans of Irish extraction, it was dedicated at a time before Ireland achieved independence but after its ultimately successful 1916 Easter Uprising.

Taras Shevchenko at P Street between 22nd and 23rd Streets (1964)

A standing portrait of the Ukrainian national poet martyred by the ruling Russians, it was sponsored by Americans of Ukrainian extraction. Placed during the height of the Cold War, it was dedicated by former President Dwight Eisenhower before a crowd of 100,000 crammed into the small triangular park. The adjoining stele is a carved relief of Prometheus, reflective of his life shortened by his harsh imprisonment.

Ukraine has a long history. Kiev on the Dnepr River, the capital of the Ukraine (meaning borderlands) was the early center of Slavic civilization. The ruler of the Kievan Rus, Vladimir the Great in 988 converted his people to the Greek Orthodox Church headquartered in Byzantium. Greek monks such as St Cyril introduced the Russian alphabet known as Cyrillic. The Mongol invasions of the 13th century pillaged Kiev. In the 15th century, rulers of the Polish-Lithuanian Commonwealth became overlords with the Ukrainians reduced to serfs working the land.

In the 17th century, the revolt against the Polish rulers led eventually to Russian "protection;" and after the partition of Poland in the late 18th century, to Russian control. 19th century Ukrainian cultural nationalism was severely suppressed by the Russian Czarist rulers. There was a transient independent Ukraine immediately following the 1918 Russian Revolution that ended with the victory of the Soviet Red Army. There was great hardship and famine in the collectivization of the farms in the early 1930s. The fullest expression of the industrialization of the Stalin 5-Year Plans was exemplified by the dams and hydro-electric plants built along the Dnepr River in the Ukraine.

Although strongly suppressed under Stalin, there remained some expression of Ukrainian nationalism that surfaced in the wake of the Nazi German occupation in 1941. Ukrainian nationalism has always been problematic. The Ukrainian uprising of the 17th century was directed primarily against the Jews as agents of the Polish overlords; it remained strongly tinged with anti-Semitism when manifested in the wake of the Russian Revolution. After the break-up of the Soviet Union in 1989, the Ukraine became once again an independent country.

Andrei Sakharov at Russia House 1800 Connecticut Avenue (1989)

One of the great intellectual figures of 20th century Russia, the bust of Sakharov sits in front of a building devoted to cultural and economic cooperation with the former Soviet republics. The son of a physicist and the post World War II leader in the development of Soviet nuclear weapons, Sakharov became persona non grata and sent into internal exile for his support for peace and human rights. He was freed by the rise to power of Mikhail Gorbachev but died in 1989 just prior to the demise of the Soviet Union he had helped to bring about on the grounds of its immorality.

The sculptor Peter Shapiro was orphaned in Russia when his parents were killed. They had immigrated to the Soviet Union to help bring about the workers' paradise that had been so cruelly promised. Shapiro was finally permitted by the Soviet authorities to return to the United States where he continued his already highly successful career.

Mahatma Gandhi at Massachusetts Avenue, Q and 21st Streets (2000)

Figure 28 - Mahatma Gandhi

Striding purposely in front of the offices of the Embassy of India, he is portrayed as on the famous Salt March to the sea in 1930. This was one of his greatest symbolic triumphs over British oppression. In defiance of the tax on salt, he led thousands to gather their own salt from the sea. The statue also shows him in his austerity wearing the simplest of garments characteristically made from homespun cotton in order to achieve independence from British manufactures.

Born in the western State of Gujarat to a family that worked for the British rulers, he was educated in law in London but, stung by the racial discrimination he experienced, fought for civil rights for Indians living in Natal in South Africa. Returning to India in 1914, he became the leader in the movement for spiritual renewal and independence from the British.

He looked for the independence movement to be rooted in Indian civilization. In his use of religious motifs to energize the masses, he transcended the diverse religious identities in his quest for religious morality. It was not enough to get rid of the English; he felt it necessary to evolve an Indian alternative to Western liberal political and economic structures. He contested the moral legitimacy of British rule that rested on the assumption of the superiority of the West.

In 1920-1922, in the first of many such episodes, India was convulsed by crescendo of strikes, boycotts and disturbances in the greatest display of mass non-cooperation and protest yet witnessed. With Gandhi arrested, more protests occurred. He emerged as the dominant figure in the political group working for independence. A new wave of non-cooperation included empty and silent streets through which the state visit of the Prince of Wales took place in 1921.

Swaraj was his motto. It meant not only self-rule but self-control or self-reliance. He preached that political emancipation lay through economic emancipation from dependency on manufactured or imported products, through ideological emancipation from the materialism of the West, and through individual emancipation from the tyranny of the self and the violence of desire. Gandhi's seemingly eccentric advocacy of the spinning wheel and the use of homespun cotton were the exemplars of this process.

The tricolor Indian flag was unfurled on January 26, 1930, the date now celebrated as Independence Day in the Republic of India. The green in the flag was for Islam and the saffron for Hinduism but the Muslim League led by Mohammed Jinnah had walked out of their meeting when a separate Muslim electorate had been rejected. The goal for Gandhi was a single and indivisible secular Indian nation that represented all communities and transcended all religious differences.

In late February 1930, Gandhi announced a new campaign. Massive civil disobedience was unleashed in the name of untaxed salt. Salt had been a state monopoly or subject to a special tax throughout much of Indian history. During the 19th century, it was a major source of revenue and subject to heavy duties by the British. Although relatively low at the time, it was a tax on all, including the poor and was deeply resented. Gandhi and his followers walked from his ashram near Ahmadabad to the Gujarat coast where the salt pans were. By picking up a handful of salt, he broke the law sanctioning the salt monopoly.

A Civil Disobedience Movement spread to the non-payment of taxes, of rents and attacks on land and property. There was also mass participation in picketing of liquor shops with alcohol forbidden by both Hinduism and Islam and boycotts of imports. As many as 92,000 persons were jailed including the entire leadership and Gandhi himself. What had occurred was a mass movement that exemplified the spirit of self-emancipation that had indeed created the conditions for independence. Independence finally came in 1947 but, despite all his efforts, it came with partition into the separate Muslim Pakistan and the Hindu majority Republic of India, sectarian violence and his own death at the hands of a Hindu assassin.

Funded by the Government of India and contributions by persons of Indian descent living in the United States, its dedication by President Bill Clinton, in the spirit of Gandhi, consisted only of throwing some rose petals.

Tomas Masaryk on Massachusetts Avenue at 23rd Street (2002)

Figure 29 - Tomas Masaryk

Born to poor parents in Moravia in 1850, he became, in 1882, a professor of philosophy at the Czech-speaking part of Charles University in Prague. Elected to the Austrian Parliament, he advocated at first merely Czech cultural freedom. In exile during World War I, he began to advocate for Czech independence after the breakup of the Austro-Hungarian Empire. He became the founder of Czechoslovakia after World War I and its first president. He is shown holding the Czech Declaration of Independence modeled after the American. Woodrow Wilson was generally acknowledged as instrumental in achieving Czech independence at the 1919 Versailles Peace Conference.

The absorption of Czechoslovakia into Soviet domination took place with the death of Thomas's son, Jan Masaryk, in 1948. The installation of this statue took place soon after the end of the Cold War. Czechoslovakia had been freed from long-term Soviet/Russian control, and the statue served as a reminder of its previous freedom under American auspices and was dedicated by President Vaclav Havel of the newly freed Czech Republic.

Victims of Communism at Massachusetts and New Jersey Avenues (2007)

Surprisingly inconspicuous and unheralded is this replica of the Statue of Liberty placed by Chinese students in Tiananmen Square in 1989. It memorializes the estimated 100 million victims of Communism. Funded by new Americans who had lived under Communist rule, it also evokes the fall of the Berlin Wall that occurred in November 1989 marking the liberation of central and Eastern Europe from Soviet Russian domination.

In the post-World War II era, a series of statues were placed near the Organization of American States (OAS) that represented the close and increasingly mutualistic relationship between the United States and the sister Latin-American republics but also the role the United States has claimed to play in history representing self-government.

General Jose de San Martin at Virginia Avenue and 24th Street (1924/1976)

A replica of the famous statue in Buenos Aires, it is a gift from the people of Argentina. The founder of Argentine independence, he carried out with his army against great odds the crossing of the Andes to bring independence to Chile and Peru. The pedestal evokes the theme of the historical role the United States has played as the representative of anti-colonialism. "..His name, like Washington, represents the American ideals of democracy, justice and liberty."

Born to a noble Spanish family in the Vice-Royalty of La Plata, he trained as a soldier in Spain. After fighting against the French in Spain during the Napoleonic Wars, he returned to Argentina in 1812 to lead in the fight for independence. His military and administrative skills helped create a disciplined army from raw, uneducated volunteers. In his quest for unity, he met in 1822 with Simon Bolivar in Guayaquil Ecuador but apparently failed since he then resigned his command and went into self-imposed exile.

Originally placed in Judiciary Square, the statue is now appropriately the central symbolic figure near other Latin American heroes placed post-World War II.

General Jose Gervasio Artigas at Constitution Avenue and 18th Street (1950)

The gift of the schoolchildren of Uruguay, it is a replica of one in Montevideo Uruguay. Standing in battle dress with his hand on the hilt of his sword, his other hand holds his hat in a sweeping gesture. He was born in 1764 in what was then called La Banda Orientale (the East Bank) of the River Plata in the Spanish-ruled Viceroyalty. He fought for Argentine independence against the British and then against the former for independence of his own province. Unsuccessful during his lifetime, he was recognized posthumously by the people of Uruguay as its founding father.

General Simon Bolivar at Virginia Avenue and 18th Street (1959)

Figure 30 - Simon Bolivar

Born in Caracas Venezuela in 1783, the son of a Spanish nobleman, Simon Bolivar received military training after schooling by his tutor in the philosophy of the Enlightenment. From 1810-1814, he fought unsuccessfully to create a republican government from the former Spanish vice-royalty of New Granada. Receiving help from Haiti, he eventually succeeded in creating by 1821 "Gran Colombia" containing much of the northern half of South America. In 1825, the former Upper Peru became the independent Bolivia, named after him. During the remainder of the decade of the 1820s, Bolivar tried to achieve a viable federation, analogous to the United States, but failed subject to the separatism that still characterizes the area.

The largest equestrian statue in the United States with his sword held high at 27 feet, he is the "George Washington of Latin America," the Liberator of six separate countries from Spanish colonial rule in the early 19th century. Donated by the Venezuelan government, he wears the medallion bestowed upon him by Lafayette and George Washington Custis, the step-son of the president. The statue was designed by Felix de Weldon, noted for the Iwo Jima Monument and is the symbolic focus around which are clustered memorials of other Latin American leaders.

Benito Juarez at Virginia and New Hampshire Avenues (1969)

A gift from the Mexican people, Benito Juarez, of pure Amerindian origin, is considered the founder of modern Mexico. Born in the southern province of Oaxaca, he was self-educated, apprenticed to a bookbinder and eventually trained in law. An advocate for the indigenous peoples and anti-clerical, he was exiled when Santa Anna came to power in 1853. He returned to power in Mexico and, with American support, became president in Mexico City in 1860.

While the United States was preoccupied by the Civil War, the suspension of payments on the foreign debt enabled Napoleon III in 1861 to justify the occupation of the capital city and the proclamation of a monarchy headed by the Habsburg Archduke Maximilian. Juarez remained in the north close to the American border and was able to regain power after the departure of the French in 1867. Despite overwhelming financial problems, he managed to maintain constitutional government until the 1870s.

The parklets created by Peter L'Enfant have served to recognize those who stood for freedom and individual liberty throughout the world as the United States has represented these principles since the founding of its capital city.

ABOUT THE AUTHOR

Dr Mark N. Ozer is a former Professor of Neurology at Georgetown University Medical School and is currently a Study Group Leader at the Osher lifelong Learning Institute at American University. There he has lectured extensively on the history of many of the great cities of the world. He has translated that interest into a series of books on Washington DC. The first entitled *Politics and Place* published in 2009 was followed by *Massachusetts Avenue in the Gilded Age* in 2010 and *Northwest Washington: Tales from West of the Park* in 2011. Born in Boston, he is a graduate of Harvard College with honors in History. He remains active in the national capital's history community with participation in the United States Capitol Historical Society, the History Society of Washington, The Association of Oldest Inhabitants, the Lincoln Group and the Cosmos Club.

TABLE OF FIGURES

WORKS CONSULTED

Alotta, Amy. *George Washington Never Slept Here.* Chicago: Bonus Books, 1993

Bednar, Michael. *L'Enfant's Legacy.* Baltimore: Johns Hopkins University Press, 2006.

Berg, Scott W. *Grand Avenues: The Story of the French Visionary who Designed Washington DC.* New York: Pantheon Books. 2007.

Bushong, William B. and Piers M. Weiss. "Rock Creek Park: Emerald of the Capital City" *Washington History* v 2 fall-winter 1990-1991 4-29.

Bushong, William. B. "Glenn Brown and the planning of Rock Creek Valley" *Washington History* v 14 spring/summer 2002 56-71

Cooling, Benjamin F. and Walter H. Owen. *Mr. Lincoln's Forts.* Shippensburg, PA: White Mane Publishing 1988.

Gilmore, Matthew and Michael Harrison. "A Catalog of Suburban Subdivisions of the District of Columbia 1854-1902" *Washington History* v 14. Fall-winter 2002-2003 p 26-55.

Goode, James. *Washington Sculpture* Baltimore: Johns Hopkins University Press, 2008.

Hagner, Alexander. "Street Nomenclature of Washington DC" *Proceedings of the Columbian Historical Society* v 7 (1904) p 237-261

Harrison, Michael. "The 'Evil of the Misfit Subdivisions': Creating the Permanent System of Highways in the District of Columbia" *Washington History.* v14 spring-summer 2002 p 26-55.

Harrison, Robert, *Washington during the Civil War and Reconstruction.* New York: Cambridge University Press, 2011

Hunt, O.E. "Defending the National Capital" In Francis Trevelyan Miller Ed. *The Photographic History of the Civil War: Forts and Artillery.* New York: Castle Books, 1957

King, LeRoy. *One Hundred Years of Capital Traction.* Washington: National Capital Trolley Museum, 1972.

Myer, Donald B. *Bridges and the City of Washington.* Washingt0on DC: Commission of Fine Arts, 1974.

Nilsson, Dexter. *The Names of Washington, DC.* Rockville, MD: Twinbrook Communications, 1998.

Ozer, Mark N. *Washington, DC: Politics and Place.* XLibris, 2010.

Washington Post (varied)

"Permanent System of Highways in the District of Columbia" In HR Report # 866 to accompany H.R. 7584 March 28th, 1892 52nd Congress 1st Session.

HR Report # 199 to accompany HR 15448 January 17th 1910.

INDEX

16365908R00105

Made in the USA
Charleston, SC
16 December 2012